CHURCH AND STATE IN AMERICA

This is an account of the ideas about and public policies relating to the relationship between government and religion from the settlement of Virginia in 1607 to the presidency of Andrew Jackson, 1829–1837. This book describes the impact of various events and legislative and judicial actions on church–state relations in America, including the English Toleration Act of 1689, the First and Second Great Awakenings, the Constitution of the United States, the Bill of Rights, and Jefferson's Letter to the Danbury Baptists. Four principles were paramount in the American approach to government's relation to religion: the importance of religion to public welfare; the resulting desirability of government support of religion (within the limitations of the political culture); liberty of conscience; and voluntarism, the requirement that religion be supported by freewill offerings, not taxation. James H. Hutson analyzes and describes the development and interplay of these principles and considers the relevance of the concept of the separation of church and state during this period.

James H. Hutson has been Chief of the Manuscripts Division at the Library of Congress since 1982. He has previously held positions as Coordinator of the American Revolution Bicentennial Programs at the Library of Congress and as lecturer at the College of William and Mary and Yale University. Among his many publications, Dr. Hutson has written *Religion and the Founding of the American Republic* (6th printing, 2002); *Forgotten Features of the Founding: The Recovery of Religious Themes in Early American History* (2003); and *The Founders on Religion* (2005).

QUAKER CONTENT

QUAKER COMPANY

CAMBRIDGE ESSENTIAL HISTORIES

Series Editor
Donald Critchlow, *St. Louis University*

Cambridge Essential Histories is devoted to introducing critical events, periods, or individuals in history to students. Volumes in this series emphasize narrative as a means of familiarizing students with historical analysis. In this series leading scholars focus on topics in European, American, Asian, Latin American, Middle Eastern, African, and world history through thesis-driven, concise volumes designed for survey and upper-division undergraduate history courses. The books contain an introduction that introduces readers to the historical event and reveals the book's thesis; narrative chapters that cover the chronology of the event or problem; and a concluding summary that provides the historical interpretation and analysis.

Titles in the Series

John Earl Haynes and Harvey Klehr, *Early Cold War Spies: The Espionage Trials that Shaped American Politics*

Maury Klein, *The Genesis of Industrial America, 1870–1920*

Church and State in America

The First Two Centuries

JAMES H. HUTSON

CAMBRIDGE
UNIVERSITY PRESS

CAMBRIDGE UNIVERSITY PRESS
Cambridge, New York, Melbourne, Madrid, Cape Town, Singapore, São Paulo, Delhi

Cambridge University Press
32 Avenue of the Americas, New York, NY 10013-2473, USA

www.cambridge.org
Information on this title: www.cambridge.org/9780521864930

© James H. Hutson 2008

This publication is in copyright. Subject to statutory exception
and to the provisions of relevant collective licensing agreements,
no reproduction of any part may take place without
the written permission of Cambridge University Press.

First published 2008

Printed in the United States of America

A catalog record for this publication is available from the British Library.

Library of Congress Cataloging in Publication Data
Hutson, James H.
Church and state in America : the first two centuries / James H. Hutson.
p.   cm.
Includes bibliographical references and index.
ISBN 978-0-521-86493-0 (hardback) – ISBN 978-0-521-68343-2 (pbk.)
1. Church and state – United States – History.   2. Christianity and politics –
United States – History.   I. Title.
BR516.H7825   2008
322′.1097309032–dc22   2007015240

ISBN   978-0-521-86493-0 hardback
ISBN   978-0-521-68343-2 paperback

Cambridge University Press has no responsibility for
the persistence or accuracy of URLs for external or
third-party Internet Web sites referred to in this publication
and does not guarantee that any content on such
Web sites is, or will remain, accurate or appropriate.

Contents

Series Editor's Foreword

The First Amendment to the Constitution, embodied in the Bill of Rights proposed by Congress in 1789 and ratified by three-fourths of the states in 1791, concerned religion. The amendment simply states, "Congress shall make no law respecting an establishment of religion, or prohibiting the free exercise thereof." This amendment prevented the federal government from establishing a national religion and allowed people to freely exercise their religious beliefs and practices. The amendment appeared straightforward, but in practice it was ambiguous and increasingly controversial.

The establishment clause – that Congress shall make no law respecting the establishment of religion – appears at a minimum to prevent the newly established federal government from granting any denomination or religious sect the privileges enjoyed in England by the Anglican Church or in other European nations by the Roman Catholic Church. The amendment was not intended, it appears, to do away with established religious denominations then exsting in the states. The question of state-established churches was left to the states.

Similarly, the free exercise clause was intended to prevent governmental persecution of dissenting religious sects and denominations as was common in England and other European countries. Congress probably intended the free exercise clause to prevent the federal government from imposing civil penalties on religious dissenters; nevertheless, even after ratification of the First Amendment, many states continued to impose civil restrictions on non-Protestants and atheists.

Throughout the nineteenth century the First Amendment drew little attention from the courts. Indeed, in the nineteenth century the Supreme Court decided only two establishment clause cases. The free exercise clause was tested in the Mormon polygamy cases, most notably, *Reynolds v. United States* (1879), in which the Court ruled that polygamous marriage was not a constitutional right founded in the First Amendment.

The shift in interpretation of the separation of church–state relations came in *Everson v. Board of Education* in 1947 when the Supreme Court considered whether a city could pay for bus transportation of school-aged children to parochial as well as pub-lic schools. The Court ruled that public funding of school buses for parochial schools was unconstitutional. Based on its review of Virginia's rejection of general taxation for the support of ministers in 1785, the Supreme Court ruled that the establishment clause was "intended to erect a 'wall of separation' between Church and State." The phrase "wall of separation" was taken from a letter Thomas Jefferson had written to a group of Baptists who opposed the state of Virginia's use of general tax funds to support established ministers. *Everson* was the first of a series of decisions undertaken by the Court in determining the precise meaning of the establishment clause and the free exercise clause.

Historian James Hutson revisits the meaning of religious toler-ation as it developed in colonial America and the early Repub-lic. Hutson presents a complex understanding of the historical background for the First Amendment. He cogently argues that the rich tradition of religious pluralism in the colonies encouraged religious toleration in America. Religious toleration, he argues, was not the founding principle of the colonies, but evolved gradually as a wide array of religious denominations and religious groups blossomed in the colonies. In accomplishing this, Hutson sheds new light on the meaning of the separation of church and state at the time of the nation's founding.

Hutson provides the reader with an historical understanding of a unique feature of the United States: religious freedom. The world he creates is far different from the secular world of the twentieth century, dominated by secular legal regimes in most countries. In this age of secularism, religious faith and secular law often appear in conflict and speak languages opaque to one another. The world that Hutson describes in colonial America was not any less complex or any less controversial than today, but the crisis of church and state that plagued Europe since the fierce religious wars of the sixteenth and seventeenth centuries appeared resolved in the American experience. The story of how this resolution came about is worth knowing because it tells us much about the founding of our nation and the meaning of toleration in this age of religious discord and hatred.

Donald T. Critchlow
General Series Editor,
Cambridge Essential Histories

CHURCH AND STATE IN AMERICA

1

The Seventeenth Century

BETWEEN THE ACCESSIONS OF JAMES I IN 1603 AND
William and Mary in 1689, Englishmen planted all the North
American colonies (save Georgia), which in 1776 declared themselves to be the United States of America. The religious map of
the colonies in 1689 resembled Joseph's coat with its multiple hues
and colors. In some colonies the state compelled obedience to one
official church; in others it was stripped of all power over its citizens'
consciences. There were colonies in which religion was regulated in
some places but not in others. And there were colonies in which the
brand of religion supported by the state varied from place to place.
In still other colonies the state refrained from regulating religion but
signaled its intention to do so in the future.

Those colonies settled after the English Civil War of the 1640s
benefited from the "new" idea of toleration, which emerged during
that conflict. Prewar colonies, on the other hand, were defiantly
intolerant, practicing a church–state policy – coercive uniformity –
that was more than a thousand years old, traceable as far back
as Christianity's ascendency in the Roman Empire in the fourth
century A.D.

The traditional, coercive policy was carried to North America in
1607 by the settlers of Virginia. At that time there were three major

religious groups in England: Anglicans, Puritans, and Catholics (whose influence had plummeted since 1559). A fourth group, no more than a speck of the English population, renounced all the nation's churches and separated itself from what it regarded as the pervasive religious rottenness by fleeing to the Netherlands; in 1620 some of these "separatists" sailed, as the Pilgrims, to Plymouth, Massachusetts. Although they were often at each others throats, Anglicans, Puritans, and Catholics agreed on a few ecclesiastical issues, one being the relationship of the state to the church. All believed that the state must assist the orthodox church in its jurisdiction, promoting its doctrines and suppressing dissent from them by force, if necessary.

Everyone in England assumed that state–church cooperation was ancient and "universal," stretching back, according to one writer, to "the Infancy of Civil Society." "Fathers of Families," this early anthropologist theorized, "who always executed the Office of Priesthood, when they advanced or were called up, to the Administration of public affairs, carried the sacred Office with them into the Magistracy . . . and continued to execute both Functions in Person." No one doubted that "all States of all Times . . . had an established religion." In his famous plea for toleration, *The Bloudy Tenent of Persecution for Cause of Conscience* (London, 1644), Roger Williams, the founder of Rhode Island, asserted that the alliance of church and state was a constant in human history and that it had constantly repressed dissent. "It is true," observed Williams, "that all magistrates do this: viz., encourage and protect the church or assembly of worshipers which they judge to be true and approve of; but not permitting other consciences than their own. It has come to pass in all ages."

There was no need for Englishmen to rummage around in the mists of prehistory to discover the origins of church–state cooperation.

They knew their Roman history and knew that during the Roman Empire "state and religion were so mixed together that it was impossible not only to have the idea of a conflict between the two but even to distinguish the one from the other." The Emperor embodied in his person the union of church and state, for he was both the chief magistrate and the chief priest, the *pontifex maximus*. The Roman practice of aligning the state with the church manifested itself as soon as Emperor Constantine made Christianity the official religion of the Empire. Only two years after his decisive victory at the Milvian Bridge (312 A.D.), Constantine and his lieutenants began "the tradition of persecution in the interests of orthodox conformity which was to mark the Christian Roman Empire and therefore its successor states, the medieval nations." The rationale for the state's employing force on behalf of the Roman Church, not always evident during the so-called Dark Ages and during periods when rogues and secular men headed the church, was the salvation of souls.

In striving to save souls, both the church and state were operating within the framework of what has been called the doctrine of exclusive salvation. This doctrine posited that there was an absolute truth necessary for salvation, that this truth was knowable, and that a particular church knew it. With unshakeable confidence, the Roman Church asserted that it was the "one universal church of the faithful, outside of which there is absolutely no salvation." The doctrine of exclusive salvation assumed, as every reader of the apostle Paul's letter to the Romans knew, that the office of the civil magistrate was instituted by God, a divine action that was considered to have authorized secular authorities to put their resources, including force, at the disposal of their clerical brethren to guide the body politic along the true path to salvation and to prevent competitors from leading the flock down the false path to perdition. The result of the doctrine was, ideally, uniformity of faith – for if all were to be saved, all must believe the same truth – and persecution of dissent. "The case for theological persecution, is unanswerable," wrote a distinguished expositor of the doctrine, "if we admit the fundamental supposition that one faith is known to be true and necessary for salvation."

The leaders of the Protestant Reformation of the sixteenth century – Luther, Calvin, Zwingli, and their associates – agreed with the Church of Rome that there was a true faith and were certain that they knew it and had rescued it from centuries of chicanery and obfuscation by the Pope and his minions. The reformers also agreed with the Church of Rome about the proper relationship between church and state. With Calvin, they held "that it is the business of government to maintain true doctrine and right worship and to suppress heresy by force." Calvin and his followers insisted on this doctrine so inflexibly that a scholar has compared them to the imperious Bishop Hildebrand, who became the mighty Pope Gregory VII in 1073. The Calvinist position has, consequently, been called the "Hildebrandine theory of the relation of church and state."

Calvinism spread from Geneva to the British Isles from the middle of the sixteenth century onward and became the dominant theological persuasion in Scotland and England (at least until the Laudean reforms of the 1630s). With it came, with modifications, the doctrine of exclusive salvation, which a scholar once claimed was "no longer tenable," in seventeenth-century England, as a "belief by minds open to reason." "Which perhaps most minds were not," the scholar immediately added, hastily reversing himself and offering as evidence of the prevailing mindset the words of a divine who in the 1630s denounced speculations about Catholics being saved as a "miserable weakness." In the 1640s, Parliament, under the control of Presbyterians, favored the "extirpation of heresie, schisme and whatsoever shall be found contrary to sound doctrine" so that "infallible and knowne truth" might prevail and promote the salvation of the English people. Theological truth was cheap in seventeenth-century England. The often humble folks who populated the unconventional and, to many, unsettling sects, which mushroomed in the 1640s, were "dogmatically certain that they alone possessed the truth," although, unlike the Calvinists, they did not want the state to impose it. At the opposite end of the intellectual scale, the deep thinker and political philosopher John Locke was not reluctant to assert in his *Letter concerning toleration* (1689), that there was a "true religion," as his enemies maliciously reminded him.

Locke's enemies were High Church Anglicans who argued into the eighteenth century that the state was justified in using force to impose uniform, true religion in England. Presbyterians leaders like Richard Baxter, who himself had been persecuted by Anglicans after the Restoration, took the same position, urging from the 1660s onward that "heretics," meaning the sects, be suppressed. It is difficult to estimate the percentage of the English population that shared these views at the end of the seventeenth century, but the number was not small, as the Sacheverell riots against dissenters in the 1710s demonstrate. Nor was the number small even in revolutionary America, for Jefferson, in his Bill for Establishing Religious Freedom (1777), railed against "legislators and rulers" for interfering in religious affairs and "setting up their own opinions and modes of thinking as the only true and infallible, and as such endeavoring to impose them" on people of other faiths. The potency of these "old-fashioned" views of church and state should not, therefore, be underestimated, as some scholars, beguiled by the growth of latitudinarian views in the late seventeenth century, have done. They were, at that time, anything but obsolete, although they certainly were not as widespread as they were at the beginning of the seventeenth century, when the settlers of Virginia and Massachusetts carried the medieval Hildebrandine convictions about church and state, as glossed by Calvin, to the New World.

The salvation of souls was not the only benefit that, in theory, might result from the application of the coercive power of the state to procure a population's adherence to a single religion. For Queen Elizabeth and many of her successors, a more tangible benefit of the state's ability to compel religious uniformity was the creation and maintenance of social and political stability. Elizabeth's great minister, Lord Burghley, stated a proposition that guided English statesmen for at least a century: There could "be no government where there was a division, and that State co[u]ld never be in Safety, where there was Tolleration of two religions. For there is no Enmytie so greate as that for religion and therefore they that differ in Service of God, can never agree in the Service of theire Contrie." A circular letter from London ministers in 1645 showed how broad the agreement with Elizabethan statesmen was. Anything short of a national uniformity in religion, the ministers claimed, would bring "divers mischiefes upon the Commonwealth. The Kingdome will be wofully weakened by scandalls and Divisions, so that Enemies both domesticall and forraigne will be encouraged to plot and practise against it."

The English Civil War of the 1640s confirmed for Charles II's ministers the truth of Burghley's observation, for they considered the conflict to have been caused by the seditious behavior of recently spawned religious sects. Religious pluralism, they concluded, had plunged the nation into chaos. Consequently, an Act of Uniformity was passed in 1662, reminiscent of Elizabeth's Act of Uniformity of 1559, whose intent was to prevent the existence of competing religious power centers by confining the public practice of religion to the Church of England. The attempt to impose religious uniformity in this instance was intended to secure and preserve public stability. The conviction that uniformity of religion was essential for political and social stability, carried to America by the first English settlers, persisted in some places until the eve of the American Revolution.

English leaders, lay and clerical, did not depend on the wisdom of the ancients or the teachings of the medieval clerics to justify the state's cooperation with the church. As citizens of a Reformed Protestant nation, they relied on a higher authority, the Bible. Multiple passages in the Old and New Testament were understood to permit – in fact, to require – that the state use all the resources at its command, including force, to assist the church. The English-men who first emigrated to America and many who came afterwards in the eighteenth century, especially Scotch-Irish Presbyterians and German Lutherans and Reformed, believed that the Scriptures plainly stated that state–church collaboration was the will of God.

The New Testament passage that was considered to require most authoritatively the state's assistance to the church was Luke 14: 16–23, Jesus' parable about a "certain man," understood to be God, who "made a great supper, and bade many." When the invited guests failed to appear, the lord ordered his servant to "Go out into the highways and hedges, and compel them to come in, that my house may be filled." The great church father, St. Augustine, argued that this parable meant that God authorized the state to use force to coerce dissidents to accept the saving mission of the Roman Church. A scholar has written that "Augustine's use of this phrase, compel them to come in, rang down through the centuries, becoming the canonical citation in the history of persecution." In the 1640s Roger

Williams complained that the Augustinian phrase was being used in England to justify state coercion of dissenters. Forty years later it enjoyed a renaissance among High Church Anglicans who urged the suppression of "schismatics" by citing with relish how authorities in Augustine's time had remorselessly compelled Donatists and other dissidents to come into the official church.

Because of its historical association with Catholic persecution, "compel them to come in," was not the weapon of choice in the arsenal of most Protestant Reformers and princes. They preferred instead an arresting passage from the Old Testament, Isaiah 49:23, in which God (as it was believed), speaking through the voice of the prophet, declared to the Church that "kings shall be thy nursing fathers and their queenes thy nursing mothers." Contradicting the traditional Catholic view that a king was a "son" or "disciple" to his priestly "father" or "master," the Isaiah passage had the potential, John Calvin perceived, to appeal to the secular ruler's pride and to arouse him to come to the defense of the young Protestant churches, struggling for existence in a sea of Catholic hostility. Calvin and his followers popularized it so successfully that it became a cliche in seventeenth-century England.

Calvin's interpretation of Isaiah 49:23 first appeared in his *Commentary* on Isaiah, published in 1551 and repeatedly reprinted thereafter. According to Calvin, princes who defended the true, reformed religion obtained "this highest pinnacle of rank, which surpasses dominion and principality of every sort, to be 'nursing-fathers' and guardians of the Church"; to be worthy of this rank princes must be "about removing superstitions and putting an end to all wicked idolatry, about advancing the kingdom of Christ and maintaining purity of doctrine, about purging scandals and cleansing from the filth that corrupts piety and impairs the lustre of Divine majesty."

Confident, apparently, of obtaining an English audience, Calvin dedicated the first edition of his *Commentary* to the young Protestant king, Edward VI, whom the Reformer urged to promote "pure doctrine." "I expressly call upon you," Calvin asserted, "or rather, God himself addresses you by the mouth of his servant Isaiah, charging you to proceed, to the utmost of your ability and power, in carrying forward the restoration of the Church. You daily read and hear that this duty is enjoined on you. More especially Isaiah, as I have said, calls *Kings the nursing fathers of the Church* (Is. xlix. 23) and does not permit them to withhold that assistance which her afflicted condition demands."

The nursing fathers metaphor, as mobilized by Calvin, was an immediate hit among Anglicans in England and Presbyterians in Scotland. James I, successively king of both realms, enthusiastically assumed the role of a nursing father to the church. In his widely read *Declaration against Vorstius* (a Dutch Socinian), James declared "that it is one of the principal parts of that duetie which appertaines unto a Christian King, to protect the trew Church within his owne Dominions, and to extirpate heresies, is a maxime without all controversie." "Those honorouable Titles . . . Nutritius Ecclesiae, Nursing father of the Church," James asserted, "doe rightly belong unto every Emperour, King, and Christian Monarch."

James's son and heir, Charles I, preened himself on being "an indulgent nursing father of the church," thus giving the metaphor the cachet of a second royal patron. In 1652 a critic charged that "it was this very Doctrine that cost the late King Charles his Crown and Life. . . . Who being flattered and bewitched into this dream of a Nursing father, and a judge of wholesome food and poyson for his people; he forced poyson for food on the Scotch Nation," provoking a war which brought him, in due course, to the scaffold.

Charles II and his post-Restoration successors fancied themselves as nursing fathers – William III, for example, was extolled as a "Nursing Father to Zion the Church of God." By the third decade of the eighteenth century, the metaphor was so popular that it was set to music by no less a composer than George Frederick Handel, who used Isaiah 49:23 as the text for one of his coronation odes (1727) for George II. A hundred years later, Anglicans were still saluting their kings, in this case, George IV, as nursing fathers of the church.

Roger Williams and other dissenters were frustrated by the power of the nursing fathers metaphor to obstruct their campaigns for liberty of conscience. "So great a weight of this controversy," he wrote in 1644, "lies upon this precedent of the Old Testament, I shall, with the help of Christ Jesus, the true King of Israel, declare and demonstrate how weak and brittle this supposed pillar of marble is to bear up and sustain such a mighty burden and weight of so many high concernments as are laid upon it." Williams's confidence was misplaced. He broke his own lance against the metaphoric pillar of marble. The metaphor was unshakeably anchored in the consciousness of the three major Protestant groups in seventeenth-century England – Anglicans, Presbyterians, and Independents (Congregationalists), precisely the groups that sent the majority of colonists to America in the seventeenth and eighteenth centuries. Here is the reason that the origin and evolution of the nursing fathers metaphor deserves attention, for these three religious groups carried the metaphor across the Atlantic. At the time of the American Revolution wherever they were in the majority – and they were in the majority in much of the country, Congregationalists in New England and Anglicans south of the Potomac – the concept of the nursing fathers – which transmitted the ancient conviction that God

commissioned the civil magistrate to establish a close, even proprietary relationship with the church and authorized him to employ
force to promote the church's doctrinal and material interests – was
the governing metaphor in church–state relations or, at the very
least, stubbornly contested the field with competing concepts.

We turn now to the actual settlement by Englishmen of the
North American continent, to Virginia and to Massachusetts Bay,
whose promoters and settlers, so different in so many ways, shared
the ideas, just described, about the relation of church and state.
Virginia was the original get-rich-quick scheme in American history, bankrolled by London investors who hoped to make a killing
by finding gold or a passage to China. Fortunes were to be wrung
from the sweat of single men, the "very excrements" of English
society, swept up from nation's slums, who died from disease and
exploitation as fast as they could be replaced by the next boatload
of benighted settlers. Like Virginia, Massachusetts Bay was settled
under the auspices of a joint-stock company, but its object was God,
not Mammon. It was, as it proudly proclaimed, a "plantation of religion," settled by families and learned ministers, which aspired, in
John Winthrop's famous words, to become a "Citty upon a Hill," a
model of church polity and practice, that would, it dared hope, if
successfully implemented in America, be imitated in England and
Protestant Europe.

A selective look at the documents generated by the government
of James I and the Virginia Company of London, the syndicate of
investors who funded the Virginia settlement, could easily create the
impression that the investors were missionaries, not money grubbers.
In charters issued to the Company in 1606, 1609, and 1612, James
congratulated the investors on "their desires for the furtherance of
so noble a work, which may, by the Providence of Almighty God,

hereafter tend to the glory of His Divine Majesty, in propagating Christian religion" to the natives "who yet live in miserable ignorance of the true knowledge and worship of God." Royal instructions issued to the Company in 1607, for the guidance of the settlers who arrived at Jamestown in May of that year, were based on the assumption that Virginia's government and church would work together to establish the true faith in colony. The instructions required the "presidents and Council and ministers" to employ "all diligence, care and respect" to "provide that the true word and service of God and the Christian faith be preached, planted and used . . . according to the doctrine, rites, and religion now professed and established within our realm." Earlier adventurers, Sir Humphrey Gilbert in 1578 and Sir Walter Raleigh in 1584, had also been ordered to ensure that "the true Christian faith, now professed in the Church of England" prevail in the colonies they proposed to establish.

The tribulations of the first years in Virginia are well known. In 1610 the remnants of the original settlers were stopped at the mouth of the James River as they were abandoning the colony. Order was reimposed by the newly arrived leaders, acting under authority of instructions issued in 1609 to a new governor, Sir Thomas Gates, putting civil and, if necessary, military administrators in control of religion in Virginia. Gates was commanded to "take principall order and care for the true and revered worship of God that his worde be duely preached and his holy sacraments administered accordinge to the constitutions of the Church of England in all fundamentall pointes." "Schisme" was to "be exemplarily punished." Public officials subsequently took care of religion in Virginia with a vengeance, regulating the conduct of both ministers and the population at large in minute detail.

A representative assembly, established in Virginia in 1619, immediately assumed control over religious affairs, passing a law requiring that "there be uniformity in our church, as near as may be, to the canons in England," decreeing mandatory church attendance for all inhabitants and regulating ministerial conduct. Having lost their money and patience, Virginia's investors ceded their interests to the crown with the result that the land became a royal colony in 1624. In 1632 the royal governor and the assembly agreed upon a statute, reiterating the requirement for uniformity, increasing ministerial salaries by the "the 20th calf, the 20th kid of goats, and the 20th pig" and requiring ministers to study the Gospels instead of wasting themselves in "excess in drinking and riot." In 1643 the assembly, at the insistence of a new governor, Sir William Berkeley, declared its support for Charles I and the Church of England in his conflict with the Parliament and the Presbyterians by passing a law declaring that the "purity of the doctrine and unity of the church" required that all nonconformists and papists be expelled from the colony. Puritan ministers who had just arrived from New England were forcibly repatriated, a decision that Governor John Winthrop of Massachusetts believed provoked God to inflict an Indian massacre on Virginia in 1644. In 1659 the assembly passed an Act for the Suppressing of Quakers, which prevented the importation of any of those "unreasonable and turbulent sort of people," ordered the expulsion of those already in Virginia, and imposed the death penalty on any Quaker, who, having been banished, returned to the colony a third time. Finally, in 1662, the assembly, imitating the Act of Conformity passed in that year by the Cavalier Parliament in England, required all ministers to conform to the Church of England on pain of expulsion from the colony. For the first time, the assembly brought the Baptists into its sights, levying fines against "schismatical persons [who] out of their averseness to the orthodox established religion, or out of new-fangled conceits of their own heretical inventions, refuse to have their children baptized."

Assessing Virginia's ecclesiastical legislation, one of the colony's first historians, Robert Beverley, writing in 1705, lamented the "mistaken Zeal" of governors and legislators, which had inposed "great restraints" and "severe Penalties" on nonconformists, prompting "many of them to flie to other Colonies," and discouraging "others of them" – potentially valuable citizens – "from going over to seat themselves" in Virginia. Looking at the same collection of laws in 1781, Thomas Jefferson was reminded of Massachusetts Bay, where the state was also in the business of promoting religious purity. That no "heretics" had been executed in Virginia, as they had been in the Bay Colony, Jefferson considered a matter of dumb luck. "If no capital execution took place here," he wrote, "as did in New-England, it was not owing to the moderation of the church, or spirit of the legislature, as may be inferred from the law itself: but to historical circumstances which have not been handed down to us."

The absence of evidence, noted by Jefferson, makes it impossible to assess the respective strength of the dual motives behind Virginia's early laws requiring the state, in its role as nursing father to the church, to police and purify religion. Whether the authors and supporters of these laws were motivated primarily by the Elizabethan conviction that uniformity in religion was necessary for social stability or by the belief that their fellow citizens could achieve eternal salvation solely and exclusively in the bosom of the "true" Church of England cannot be known. Both sentiments were doubtless at work.

Virginia's northern neighbors in the Massachusetts Bay Colony left no mystery about the rationale for their ecclesiastical legislation, for they were eager, almost obsessively so, to explain their views on church and state. The unconventional character of Massachusetts's church government (as opposed to its doctrines) and the incessant attacks upon it by English opponents put the leaders of the

Bay Colony in a permanent posture of self-justification. The people of Massachusetts were Puritans, an imprecise term of oppro-
brium, tacked onto those who took their religion too seriously for
many Englishmen. They believed that the true church consisted of
covenanted communities of men and women who had received –
and could publicly prove that they had received – saving grace.
These saints, as they were derisively called by their critics, formed
individual communities of faith that functioned independently of any
hierarchy, be it of bishops or presbyters. Historians have called this
form of church polity nonseparating Congregationalism because the
Puritans settlers of Massachusetts contended that they remained
within the communion of the Church of England, even though,
according to Roger Williams, they privately denounced it as a
"whore."

In the 1620s the prospect of resolving quarrels between the
Puritans and the Anglican hierarchy about reforming the Church of
England began to look hopeless. Persecuted and threatened with
"extirpation from the Earth," Puritan leaders began planning a mi-
gration to Massachusetts Bay, which commenced in 1630 and
reached 20,000 men, women, and children by 1643. Once "your
feete are safely set on the shores of America," the Puritan settlers
were urged to "provoke . . . all that are in authority to caste downe
their Crownes at the feet of Christ, and take them up again at his command under his Standard as nursing Fathers and nursing Mothers
to the Churche."

The nonseparating Congregationalists who arrived in Massachusetts Bay were as certain as Calvin and Luther had ever been that
they were in possession of religious truth. Their "greatest comfort,"
they said, was "that we have here the true Religion and holy Ordi-
nanaces of Almightie God." "If the Lord Jesus were here himselfe

in person," one of their leaders declared, he would attest to their fidelity to his doctrines. Preaching was, for the Puritans, the divinely appointed path to eternal life; it was "the chief ordinary means ordered by God for the converting, edifying, and saving of the souls of the elect." Since it was the duty of the civil authorities, who were called, in proper Calvinist fashion, "God's viceregents on earth," to promote the "salvation of inferiors by their authority," they must ensure that the ministers preached the pure and undiluted truth. Should a magistrate fail to secure sound preaching, he would betray his divinely ordained trust to be a "nursing father of the church," a term which the New Englanders wrote into their authoritative Cambridge Platform of 1648. According to John Cotton, New England's most celebrated theologian, it was the magistrates' duty "as nursing fathers of the church, not only to feed, but also to correct, and therefore, consequently bound to judge what is true feeding and correcting: and, consequently, all men are bound to submit to their feeding and correcting."

Those who did not care to dine on the true religion served by New England's nursing fathers had "free liberty to keep away from us," wrote Nathaniel Ward in 1647. Like the Virginians, the Puritans expelled those who refused to keep away. The magistrates of Massachusetts Bay were determined to suppress all "infecting, infringing, impugning or impairing principles," not only because they jeopardized the salvation of souls but because religious pluralism disturbed the social order. A dissenter from the orthodox religion, declared John Winthrop, "cannot stand with the peace of any state."

Between 1630 and 1660, authorities in Massachusetts arrested and expelled – or threatened to arrest and expel – representatives of virtually every shade of religious opinion in the English-speaking world: Antinomians, Presbyterians, Separatists, Baptists, and fringe groups like Ranters, Familists, Adamites, and Gortoneans. Particularly noxious to the Massachusetts authorities were the Quakers. Against these "Pests," the colony passed laws, little different from those in Virginia, banishing them and imposing the death penalty – by a single vote, it should be added – if they returned a third time. One Quaker, Mary Dyer, returned a fourth time. She and three other Quakers, seeking martyrdom, were hanged in Boston between 1659 and 1661.

No other Puritan colony established before the outbreak of the English Civil War in 1642, executed "heretics," not because they were opposed, in principle, to doing so, but because, as Jefferson surmised about Virginia, the circumstances did not present themselves. Connecticut (founded as a spin-off from Massachusetts between 1633 and 1636), New Haven (founded in 1638 and united with Connecticut in 1662), and Plymouth (founded in 1620 and united with Massachusetts in 1691) formed with the Bay Colony and Virginia a phalanx of states, different in significant ways, but all dedicated to the same ancient idea, stretching back beyond the medieval Catholic Church to the fourth-century Roman Empire – the idea that the state must embrace the church and impose its truth, uniformly, wherever its writ ran.

One other colony – Maryland – was founded in North America before civil war began in England in 1642, and there the ancient ideas about state–church collaboration did not immediately gain a foothold. Much else was distinctive about Maryland. It was sponsored, funded, and governed, not by a joint-stock company, as Virginia and Massachusetts had been, but by a single individual, a proprietor. Proprietorship was an entrepreneurial vehicle employed by the English crown to shift the expenses of colonization to a private individual, usually a royal favorite, or to a group of courtiers. It was introduced in Barbados in 1629 and became popular after 1660, being employed in Carolina, New York, New Jersey, and Pennsylvania. The Maryland proprietorship differed from its namesakes in one striking way: It was vested by Charles I in men of the despised Catholic faith, the Calvert family.

George Calvert, created Lord Baltimore on the Irish establishment in 1625, was a court favorite, despite being unapologetically Catholic. An enthusiast for North American colonization, Calvert tried and failed to found a colony in Newfoundland. He then attempted to settle in Virginia in 1629, but anti-Catholic sentiment there compelled him to leave, sentiment so strong that a few years later Virginians declared that "they would rather knock their cattle on the head than sell them to Maryland." Returning to England, Calvert used his influence at court to obtain a charter for Maryland, which was issued June 30, 1632, soon after his death. Calvert's son, Cecilius, became the proprietor and attempted to establish in Maryland a feudal seignory, as his charter gave him the authority to do. Calvert's charter contained clauses that pointed toward an establishment of the Church of England in the colony, but his objective was to make Maryland a refuge for the persecuted Catholics of England. Some historians have argued that Calvert's principal purpose in colonizing Maryland was to make money "since he wrote constantly of profit and loss and of prospects of future gain," an observation that would apply with equal force to William Penn, whose devotion to the spiritual welfare of his coreligionists has never been challenged.

Success in Maryland, however defined by Calvert, depended on social harmony, which was far from assured since the first settlers were a mixture of Catholics and Protestants, who might be expected to carry Old World animosities to the New. Protestants apparently outnumbered Catholics from the beginning. Settlement began in 1634. By 1641 a Jesuit priest caustically estimated that "three parts of the people in four at least are heretics [i.e., Protestants]." Calvert's best hope for stability lay in promoting mutual forbearance in the colony, which he encouraged by instructing his first governor, his brother Leonard, to see that "no scandal or offense . . . be given to any of the protestants" and that "all acts of the Roman Catholic religion be done privately" and that Catholics "be silent" on religious issues. Calvert's policy established a de facto religious liberty, although he apparently acted for pragmatic reasons and did not articulate any principled defense of his actions. The peaceful coexistence of Catholics and Protestants in Maryland without government interference was something new under the sun, not only in North America but in England itself.

The success of the Maryland experiment could not, however, survive the shock of the English Civil War, which plunged the nation into eighteen years of revolutionary turmoil (1642–1660). The Civil War was a watershed in Anglo-American religious history, which led to the introduction, first in England and then in the North American colonies, of the principle of religious toleration. As soon as Charles I's opponents arrayed themselves against him, they began to disagree over the legitimacy of using the state to impose an orthodox religion. As the war progressed and as new religious sects began to multiply, the disputes became more acrimonious and led to the introduction of religious toleration, not least because Oliver Cromwell and the New Model Army, the source of power in England, supported it. Toleration meant different things to different people, but at a minimum it was intended to permit multiple groups of Protestants to practice their religion without molestation by the state. The attractiveness of the concept of toleration must not, however, be exaggerated. A scholar has recently cautioned that "although the years 1640–1660 resounded with the controversy over toleration, those who believed in tolerating diversity among Christians were never more than a minority."

The restoration of the Stuart monarchy in 1660 led to a reaction in religious policy, when a vindictive, Anglican-dominated Parliament attempted to reimpose true, uniform worship under the authority of the Church of England and sanctioned persecution, some of it savage, of religious dissent. Yet the idea of toleration had gained a following among England's elites, so pronounced that in 1675 William Penn claimed that arguments for it had "often and excellently" been made "by men of wit, learning and conscience." Charles II and James II supported toleration for political and economic, if not for principled, reasons. Some of each king's cronies, acting as proprietors, introduced the idea of toleration into projects they sponsored to colonize North America. It is a fact, often overlooked, that after 1642, every colony established in North America was constituted with some measure of toleration built into its governing structure.

The English Civil War initially brought Maryland not toleration, but a violent revival of the old idea of the hegemony of the one true religion. In 1645 a self-appointed champion of the colony's "oppressed" Protestants, Richard Ingle, invaded the colony to liberate it from a "tyrannical governor and the papists." Ingle expelled all the Catholics he could find, destroyed the Jesuit residence at St. Ingoes, forcing the priests to flee to Virginia, where they mysteriously disappeared, and ravaged the colony for two years, a period subsequently known as the "plundering time."

Observing this sectarian rampage from England even as he worried that militant Protestants in Parliament, flushed with victory over Charles I, might confiscate his proprietorship, Cecilius Calvert in

1649 sent to the colony for passage by the assembly his famous "Act Concerning Religion," in which he granted the "free exercise" of religion to Marylanders. Whether Calvert acted to curry favor with Cromwell and his followers or whether he was reaffirming a consistent commitment to religious liberty has been debated by historians. What is clear is that, living in London, Calvert "realized," in the words of a distinguished scholar, "that there was a growing interest at large in a new idea – the idea of liberty of conscience." This statement is true in a qualified sense. Cromwell and his allies were apostles of what they defined as toleration, but were far from being advocates of liberty of conscience in its unrestricted modern sense. Nor was Calvert, for his Act Concerning Religion limited the free exercise of religion to those in Maryland "professing to believe in Jesus Christ" and imposed the death penalty on any who should "deny the holy trinity the father sonne and holy Ghost." Calvert, in short, demanded that the state perform its traditional role of promoting religious truth and suppressing error, expanding the truth to be protected from one particular confession to Trinitarian Christianity in general. Calvert in 1649 granted religious liberty to Trinitarian Christians, but he coupled this new idea with the old concept of the state as a compulsive nursing father, protecting religious truth and, in this case, exterminating error on the gallows. The distance from his "liberal"policy to the modern conception of liberty of conscience is immense.

The fragility of religious liberty in Maryland was revealed by a "Puritan Rebellion," which followed closely on the heels of "Ingle's Rebellion." Governor Berkeley of Virginia, perennially purifying the Old Dominion of "sectaries and schismatics," had "driven," as he boasted, a group of Puritans from the colony in 1649. Settling near present-day Annapolis, the Puritans obtained control of the government in 1654, after defeating Calvert's supporters in armed combat. They repealed the "Act Concerning Religion," outlawed "prelacy or popery" and expelled the Jesuits priests who had returned to the colony, forcing them to live in exile, "in a little low hut, like a cistern or tomb." Calvert regained control of Maryland in 1657 and reinstated the Act Concerning Religion, which remained in force until the Glorious Revolution of 1688. Marylanders now enjoyed a modified freedom of religion, restricted to Trinitarian Christianity, and violated on occasion, as when forty Quakers were fined and horsewhipped in 1658; under this regimen a "polyglot" religious community developed, three-quarters of whom, according to Lord Baltimore's estimate in 1676, were "Presbiterians, Independents, Anabaptists and Quakers," the remainder being Roman Catholics, Anglicans, and Lutherans, joined a few years later by a group of mystics, the Labadists.

The first colony approved by English officials after the beginning of the civil war in 1642 was Rhode Island or, as it was called at its inception, "Providence Plantations in Narragansett." Unlike Maryland and the post-1660 colonies, Rhode Island was not the brainchild of a profit-seeking proprietor well connected at the English court. Its founder was Roger Williams, expelled from Massachusetts in 1636 for religious nonconformity and extolled for decades in the nation's schoolbooks as America's foremost "Apostle of Religious Liberty." Williams conceived of Rhode Island as a "shelter for persons distressed for conscience," to which idea he gave the widest possible scope. "I commend that man," he said, "whether Jew or Turk, or Papist, or whatever, that steers no otherwise than his conscience does." Whatevers of every sort congregated in Rhode Island, including religious zealots and oddballs who had been expelled from both Massachusetts Bay and Plymouth. In the eyes of her orthodox

Puritan neighbors, Williams's colony was the "the latrina of New England."

Williams's commitment to "soul liberty" was based on his view that the state had authority only over men's "bodies and goods"; intangible, "spiritual" matters he considered to be completely off limits to the civil magistrate. As a result, no religion of any kind was established in Rhode Island, an arrangement that Williams succeeded in having confirmed on a trip to in England in 1644. When he arrived in London, Charles I had fled the city, and the government was in the hands of Parliament. Williams appeared before the committee for foreign plantations, which was dominated by Oliver Cromwell and other friends of toleration for "tender consciences." The committee granted him a patent (not a charter, as is frequently asserted) which secured religious liberty by an act of "intentional omission" (i.e., by the absence of any mention of religion). The patent has been compared to the original, unamended Constitution of the United States, which members of the Philadelphia Convention of 1787 believed secured religious liberty by withholding from the national government any power to act on the subject.

The restoration of Charles II in 1660 raised questions about the validity of the 1644 patent, causing Rhode Islanders to commission John Clarke, a Newport Baptist minister who had remained in England after accompanying Williams to London in 1651, to secure a charter from the king. Against formidable odds, Clarke succeeded. In January 1662 he petitioned Charles II's ministers, informing them that his fellow citizens "have it much in their hearts, if they may be permitted, to hold forth a lively experiment, that a flourishing and civil state may stand, yea and best be maintained, and that among English spirits, with a full liberty in religious commitments." On July 8, 1663, the royal government granted a charter to "the colony of Rhode Island and Providence Plantations," which declared that "noe person . . . shall bee in any wise molested, punished, disquieted or called in question for any difference in opinions in matters of religion which doe not actually disturb the civil peace of our sayd colonye; but that all and everye person and persons may . . . freeley and fullye have and enjoy his and their own judgments and consciences in matters of religious concernments."

Partisans of the Calvert family, generally Catholics or Marylanders, often both, have challenged Williams's credentials as the architect of American religious liberty, alleging that he was an anti-Catholic and anti-Quaker bigot. Williams, it is true, would have disarmed Catholics and required them to wear "distinctive clothing." Nor did he conceal that he "hated" the theology of the Quakers, denouncing them as "greedy Wolves, devouring the souls of the . . . innocent lambs and sheep of Christ," as "filthy dreamers as . . . Monstrous, and Blasphemous as the Papists," who were, nevertheless, welcome to live in peace in Rhode Island. In 1672, at the age of seventy-two, Williams rowed eighteen miles to Newport to conduct a three-day disputation with Quaker leaders, which resulted in his vituperative pamphlet, *George Fox Digg'd Out of his Burrowes* (1676). Williams offered no apology for conducting "spiritual warfare" against the Quakers, for he was, after all, as much a Puritan as his Massachusetts adversaries, committed to defending theological truth and combating theological error, differing from them only in his choice of weapons, employing the "spiritual sword" rather than the civil one.

Decisive objections have also been made to the claims of Williams's admirers that he influenced Jefferson, Madison, and other kindred spirits in their campaigns against the established churches of their day. Recent scholars have pointed out that Williams's writings, published in England, were unknown to Americans of the revolutionary generation. Had they been known, his principal argument for religious liberty would have been unintelligible, or at least irrelevant, to the Founders. Williams based his case for religious liberty on typology, an old and controversial method of scriptural interpretation. Most of his contemporaries believed that events and individuals in the Old Testament were "types" or models for similar events and people in the New Testament. The theory secured for the Old Testament a continuing relevance to the Christian community and legitimatized for the seventeenth-century passages such as the "the nursing father" in Isaiah 49:23 as appropriate scriptural guidance on church–state relations. Williams argued, on the contrary, that the coming of Christ had nullified the relevance of Old Testament models. Old Testament Canaan, he insisted, "was not a pattern for all lands. It was a nonesuch, unparalleled, unmatchable." The true pattern for church–state relations, therefore, was that prescribed in the New Testament by Jesus, who repudiated all church–state connections by announcing that his kingdom was "not of this world." Williams's abstruse, scriptural arguments, Perry Miller has written, "exerted little or no influence on institutional developments in America; only after the concept of liberty for all denominations triumphed on wholly other grounds did Americans look back on Williams and invest him with his ill fitting halo."

Williams did, however, advance one argument for religious liberty that revealed him to be in tune with the most progressive secular thinkers of his generation: the idea that toleration was good for the economy. Wrote Williams in his *Bloudy Tenent of Persecution*: "let conscience and experience speak how in not cutting off their many religions, it has pleased God not only not to be provoked, but to prosper the state of the United Provinces, our next neighbors, and that to admiration." Here Williams addressed one of the major geopolitical puzzles of the age; how had the tiny Dutch Republic emerged as a major rival to England in commerce, wealth and military power? Pundits wrestled with the problem, especially in the 1660s and 1670s, and reached a consensus that religious liberty was responsible for their little neighbor's surprising ascendancy. In his widely read *Observations upon the United Provinces of the Netherlands* (1673), Sir William Temple concluded that the "vast growth of their trade and riches, and consequently the strength and greatness of their state" could be attributed to the wisdom of the Dutch in granting "impartial protection" to all religions in their country. William Penn was among those who agreed. Why, he asked, was the Netherlands, "that bog of the world, neither sea nor dry land, now the rival of the tallest monarchs." Because, Penn answered, the Dutch "cherished [their] people, whatsoever were their opinions, as the reasonable stock of the country, the heads and hands of her trade and wealth; and making them easy in the main point, their conscience, she became great by them; this made her fill with people, and they filled her with riches and strength."

"That trade depends much upon Liberty of Conscience" became a truism in Restoration England. Policymakers were certain that "imposing upon Conscience in matters of religion is a mischief unto Trade, transcending all other whatsoever." This conviction had an application beyond direct competition with the Dutch in Europe, for it was widely assumed that settlers would not submit to the primitive conditions in the North American colonies if their religious beliefs were at risk. "Indulgence must be granted in matter of opinion," wrote Sir William Petty, if settlers were to be attracted to the colonies, there to produce the raw materials, required for a thriving English transatlantic trade. That these settlers would also be buyers of lands offered for sale by proprietors of new colonies was self-evident, and therefore the profit motive became a powerful incentive, impelling promoters of colonization to offer religious liberty to attract prospective purchasers of their property.

The first example in Restoration England of religious liberty granted on economic grounds was the recently conquered colony of Jamaica, whose governor was instructed in 1661 to grant toleration to all Protestants. An expert on seventeenth-century imperial history has suggested that the policy in Jamaica influenced the granting of liberty of conscience in the Rhode Island charter of 1663, for "if Jamaica and the new proprietary colonies were to enjoy freedom of worship, why should Rhode Island not enjoy it also?"

A better documented instance of the interplay of economic and other motives in securing liberty of conscience in the new, post-Restoration proprietary colonies was the case of "Carolana," the area that became the royal provinces of North and South Carolina in the eighteenth century. In 1663 Charles II granted a charter to Carolina to eight favorites, who were long-time enthusiasts for and investors in foreign trade and North American colonization. They assisted their royal patron by serving on committees of the privy council, concerned with trade and "foreign plantations," in which positions they were "instrumental in formulating trade policy for the nation and in directing naval affairs."

A leader of the group of eight was Anthony Ashley Cooper, who became the first earl of Shaftesbury in 1672. A Presbyterian who fought in the parliamentary army against Charles I and who served on the council of state during the Cromwellian period, Cooper had long supported toleration as a matter of right. He was also convinced of its economic advantages, writing in 1668 a pro-toleration memorial, whose sentiments were incorporated into a House of Lords report that declared "that ease and relaxation in ecclesiastical matters will be the means of improving the trade of this kingdom." Cooper's fellow proprietors favored toleration on economic grounds only. The difference between him and his associates is well described by Sir George Clark: "to those who most surely believe in it, toleration ... is the essence of religion itself, and there were some who so understood it, but even some of these, and still more the mass of moderate and fair-minded men, were apt to argue for it on the mundane ground that it was good for trade."

These "moderate" men, who controlled the fledgling imperial bureaucracy of the Stuarts, issued instructions to colonial governors of the following tenor: "because we are willing to give all possible encouragement to persons of different persuasions in matters of religion to transport themselves thither with their stocks, you are not to suffer any man to be molested or disquieted in the exercise of his religion." Their like-minded successors issued what, beginning in the 1680s, became standing instructions to all royal governors in North America, ordering them "to permit a liberty of conscience to all persons EXCEPT PAPISTS, so they be contended with a quiet and peaceable enjoyment of the same, not giving offense or scandal to the government." This policy continued as long as the British writ ran in North America. In 1752, for example, the Board of Trade declared that "a free Exercise of Religion is so valuable a branch of true liberty, and so essential to the enriching and improving of a trading Nation, it should ever be held sacred in his Majesty's Colonies." Colonialism and capitalism were, in the early British Empire, engines of liberty – at least, in the religious sphere.

The eight "Lords and Proprietaries" of Carolina, who received royal charters in 1663 and 1665, acted like rulers of modern banana republics by issuing and revising between 1669 and 1698 four "fundamental" constitutions. These constitutions are monuments to the impracticality of intellectuals. Based on the ideas of the political philosopher James Harrington, they envisioned a feudal, manorial world of "landgraves," "caciques," and serfs, which had no chance of succeeding in frontier conditions of the New World. An intellectual greater than Harrington, John Locke, played a role in the composition of the most famous of the fundamental constitutions, that of 1669.

Locke's unpublished writings show that by 1667 he had become a convert to religious toleration. In the same year, he joined Shaftesbury's household as a physician, secretary and confidant. The two men collaborated on the fundamental constitution of 1669, although Locke may merely have served as a clerk, reducing Shaftesbury's ideas to writing. The 1669 document was one of the most liberal official instruments of the seventeenth century. It expanded and added specifics to the language of the 1663 and 1665 royal charters, which were already generous enough. In the 1665 document, for example, Charles II, in language lifted from the Rhode Island charter of 1663, permitted the proprietors to grant "such Indulgencies and dispensations" in religious practices as they "in their discretion, think fit and reasonable," ordering that "no person or persons unto whom such liberty shall be given shall be any way molested, punished, disquieted, or called in question for any differences in opinion or practice in matters of religious concernment ... but all and every such Person and Persons may, from time to time, and at all times, freely and quietly have and enjoy his and their Judgements and Consciences in matters of religion throughout all the said Province or Colony."

The 1669 constitution improved upon these terms by granting liberty of conscience to Jews, anti-Trinitarian Christians, and any seven people who formed a church that believed in one God who was "publicly to be worshipped." "No man of any other Church or profession," the constitution stipulated, "shall disturb or molest any Religious Assembly" and "No person whatsoever shall disturb, molest, or persecute another for his speculative opinions in Religion or his way of worship."

The 1669 constitution evidently troubled a majority of the eight proprietors, who feared that its terms were so open-ended that they would offend the English Parliament, which from 1662 onward was committed to imposing religious uniformity at home. Consequently, in 1670 they amended it by inserting a clause establishing the Church of England, when conditions in Carolina permitted, although dissenting colonists were to enjoy broad toleration under the new dispensation. The 1670 establishment clause continued in force in the last two proprietary constitutions of 1682 and 1698.

For decades the proprietors and their lieutenants in North and South Carolina made no efforts to promote religion of any kind in the colonies, with the result that up to the Glorious Revolution of 1688 and beyond the settlers enjoyed religious liberty in the shadow of a prospective establishment of the Church of England. The prevailing freedom of religion brought settlers of various persuasions to the Carolinas. In North Carolina Quakers flourished. Presbyterians and Anglicans were present as were others whose religious allegiances were a mystery to observers attempting to describe them. South Carolina received a substantial contingent of Anglicans from Barbados as well as Presbyterians, Baptists, French Calvinists (Huguenots), and Quakers. Religious pluralism in proprietary Carolina was every bit as robust as it was in proprietary Maryland.

The next proprietary colony established after the restoration of Charles II was the work of the King's brother, James, Duke of York, the future James II (1685–8). James was the Lord High Admiral of England's navy and an implacable foe of the Dutch. In 1664 he dispatched a fleet to North America, which captured New Amsterdam without a shot. The conquered Dutch colony was renamed New York. James became its sole proprietor. Like his friends, the Carolina proprietors, James wanted to enrich himself from his new proprietorship. He shared the Carolinians' conviction that religious liberty was a precondition for profit in North American investing. "Forcing consciences," James declared, was contrary "to the interests of government, which it destroys by spoiling trade, depopulating countries, and discouraging strangers." Consequently, James consistently promoted freedom of worship. In 1665 his first governor, Richard Nicholls, promulgated "the Duke's Laws," which established a complicated religious regime, which has been described as a "local option" arrangement and as a "nondenominational state church." Under this scheme, the majority of voters in each town could make the church of its choice the legally established church and support it with tax revenues, permitting the minority to constitute its own church and worship without government interference. In theory, the New York could become the home of a kaleidoscope of different official churches, as actually happened in parts of Long Island.

In 1674 James reiterated his commitment to religious liberty by instructing Governor Andros to "permit all persons of what religion soever, quietly to inhabitt within the precincts of your jurisdiccon, without giving them any disturbance or disquiet whatsoever, for or by reason of their differing opinions in matters of Religion." The result of James's policy was a luxuriant pluralism that amazed some of the deputies he sent out from England, although they would not have been so surprised had they known that as early as 1642 eighteen different languages were spoken in the province. Wrote Governor

Thomas Dongan in 1687: "New York has first a Chaplain belonging to the Fort of the Church of England; secondly a Dutch Calvinist, thirdly a french Calvinist, fourthly a Dutch Lutheran – Here bee not many of the Church of England; few roman Catholicks; abundance of Quaker preachers men and women especially; Singing Quakers; Ranting Quakers; Sabbatarians; Antisabbatarians; Some Anabaptists; some Independents; some Jews; in short of all sorts of opinion there are some."

Barely three months after James acquired New York, he confounded both his lieutenants in the new colony and historians of the period by giving away the rich lands south of Manhattan, the area between the Hudson and Delaware Rivers, to two old friends, John, Lord Berkeley, and Sir George Carteret, who were now associated with him in the administration of the Royal Navy and who had earlier distinguished themselves as commanders in the military forces of Charles I. Already proprietors of Carolina, Berkeley and Carteret became in June 1664 proprietors of New Jersey. Like their brother proprietors, they wanted to make money in North America. According to a leading historian of New Jersey, they were "essentially real estate promoters, anxious to attract settlers to their domain in order that they might derive a profitable revenue from land rents. Designedly, then, they offered extremely liberal political and religious privileges to prospective immigrants."

The religious privileges offered to the settlers of New Jersey were described in a document that was copied from Concessions made by the Carolina proprietors, January 7, 1665, to a group of Barbadians intending to settle in the Cape Fear region of that colony. The "Concessions and Agreement of the Lords Proprietors of New-Caesaria, or New Jersey," issued by Berkeley and Carteret, February 10, 1665, stipulated that "no person or persons . . . shall be any ways molested, punished, disquieted, or called in question for any differences in opinion or practice in matters of religious Concernment . . . but that all and every such person and persons may, from time to time, and at all times, freely and fully have and enjoy his and their Judgments and Consciences in matters of religion throughout all the said province." The Concessions then added this enigmatic clause: "We do hereby grant unto the General Assembly of the said Province power, by act, to constitute and appoint such and so many Ministers or Preachers as they shall think fit, and to establish their maintenance; Giving Liberty besides to any person or persons to keep and maintain what preachers or Ministers they please."

Were the proprietors laying the groundwork for the establishment of the Church of England in New Jersey as the 1670 amendment to the Carolina constitution did in that colony? Or did they envision a "local option" scheme along the lines established by the Duke's Laws in neighboring New York? Or were they anticipating something like the plural establishments, proposed in some American states in the 1780s, in which the state was expected to provide, impartially, financial support to several different denominations? The existing evidence does not permit an answer. All that is clear is that the New Jersey proprietors were prepared to permit the state to take an active role in religious affairs in their colony.

As in Carolina, neither the New Jersey proprietors nor assembly concerned themselves with religion, with the result that the settlers, as in Carolina, enjoyed unrestrained religious freedom. In that environment the pattern in other proprietary colonies – a lively pluralism – repeated itself. Congregationalists, Baptists, and Quakers arrived in New Jersey from Long Island and southern New England; Dutch Reformed, from New York; and Presbyterians, from Scotland.

The team of Berkeley and Carteret dissolved in 1674, when Berkeley sold his share of the proprietorship to a Quaker, John Fenwick, acting on behalf of another Quaker, Edward Byllinge, whose financial affairs were so embarrassed that William Penn and two other Quakers were forced to take control of his interests. In the meantime, the New Jersey proprietorship was divided, in 1676, into western and eastern sections; Byllinge's share was situated in West New Jersey, which became a Quaker refuge, controlled by Quaker proprietors (at one time as many as forty-eight). The Quaker settlement of West New Jersey is usually considered a dress rehearsal for the launching, a few years later, of William Penn's larger Quaker colony across the Delaware River, but the West Jersey experiment is of interest because the proprietors issued a memorable testimonial to religious liberty, ascribed by most historians to Penn himself, in the form of "Concessions and Agreements," granted to the settlers of Burlington in 1677. The Concessions declared that "no men, nor number of men, upon earth, hath power or authority to rule over men's consciences in religious matters . . . that no person or persons whatever within the said Province, at any time or times hereafter, shall be any ways upon any pretence whatsoever, called into question, or in the least punished or hurt, either in person, estate, or priviledge, for the sake of his opinion, judgment, faith or worship towards God in matters of religion. But that all and every such person, and persons, may from time to time, and at all times, freely and fully have, and enjoy his and their judgments, and exercise of their consciences in matters of religious worship throughout all the said Province."

Quakers quickly moved from England to West New Jersey because of the severe and unremitting persecution they suffered in the mother country. The Quakers, or Religious Society of Friends (as they preferred to be called), coalesced in England in 1652 around a charismatic leader, George Fox. Today many scholars regard them as radical Puritans, an identification both groups would have loathed. This affiliation is credible, however, because the Quakers carried many Puritan convictions to extremes. They stretched the sober deportment of the Puritans into a glorification of "plainness." Theologically, they expanded the Puritan concept of a church of individuals regenerated by the Holy Spirit to the idea of the indwelling of the Spirit or the "light of Christ" in every person. Salvation was available to anyone who would open himself or herself – Quakers scandalized their contemporaries by stressing the equality of the sexes – to the power of God within. "The whole tendency of their preaching," wrote the famous Quaker apostate, George Keith in 1702, "was that the Light within every Man was sufficient to his salvation without anything else."

"Without anything else" is what got the Quakers in trouble with the authorities, for they believed that the Inner Light made most of organized religion irrelevant. The sacraments were considered to be superfluous, as was a trained ministry. The Bible was not binding, for it was only a "declaration of the fountain, not the fountain itself." To their contemporaries the Quakers seemed to be scheming to purify Christianity out of existence. As a result, open season was declared upon them in the press and in the courts. Typical of the literary tirades against them was John Brown's *Quakerisem the pathway to Paganisme* (1678), in which Quaker convictions were reviled "as the dreadfulest delusion of Satan, and of darkness, caused by the Prince of darkness, that ever was heard of in the Christian world." William Penn was accused of being a "greater AntiChrist than Julian the Apostate."

Many thought that the Quakers deserved whatever physical violence the state inflicted. What if a Quaker received 117 lashes on the bare back; had not he and his companions "endeavoured to beat the Gospel ordinances black and blew?" By 1680 ten thousand

Quakers had been imprisoned in England and 243 had died from torture and imprisonment in the King's jails, trauma compared to which the suffering of the Puritans who emigrated to New England was a drop in the bucket. This reign of terror galvanized William Penn into action on behalf of his fellow Friends. The son of Admiral William Penn, naval commander of the expedition against the Spanish West Indies in 1655, and later a commander in the Dutch Wars of the 1660s, young Penn used his navy connections to gain the friendship of the Carolina proprietors and of James, Duke of York. To erase a debt of £16,000, owed by the crown to Penn's father, who had paid sailors' salaries from his own pocket, Charles I, on March 4, 1681, issued a charter to William Penn, making him proprietor of Pennsylvania. Settlement began in 1682. By 1685 as many as eight thousand Quakers had settled in Pennsylvania.

Though a great and authentic religious leader, Penn had much in common with the other seventeenth-century North American proprietors. Like them, he advocated religious toleration as a stimulant to economic growth and made no secret that he intended to profit personally from the settlement of Pennsylvania. For Penn, spiritual and economic prosperity were in no way incompatible. Where Penn differed from his brother proprietors, with the exception of his friend Shaftesbury, was in his conviction that religious liberty was mandated by New Testament Christianity. Employing "external force in matters of faith," Penn was certain, was "no less than the overthrow of the whole Christian religion." He was always ready with a long list of New Testament passages to prove his point. His favorite verse, which runs like a leitmotiv through his writings, was John 18:36 in which Christ declared: "My kingdom is not of this world, for then would my servants fight for me." In a characteristic gloss, Penn explained that "because the kingdoms of this world are evidently set up by and maintained by worldly force, and that he will have no worldly force used in the business of his kingdom, that therefore it is not of this world. Consequently, those that attempt to set up his kingdom by worldly force, or make that their pretence to use it, are none of his servants." The "gross Apprehension of the nature of Christ's Kingdom," Penn informed the Prince of Orange, accounted for the mistakes "about the means of promoting it, else were it not Credible, that men should think, Clubs, Prisons & Banishments the proper Mediums of inlightening the Understanding."

Between 1681 and 1683 Penn promulgated a series of charters for the government of Pennsylvania in some of which he incorporated his views on the religion and government. He is known to have studied the constitutions of Carolina. Article 35 of the Penn's 1682 Laws Agreed upon in England, in which religious liberty was granted to any one who believed in God, be he Catholic, Jew, Muslim, or anti-Trinitarian Christian, may have been patterned after the 1669 Carolina constitution, written by Shaftesbury with the assistance of Penn's friend, John Locke. Article 35 stated that all persons living in Pennsylvania

> who confess and acknowledge the one Almighty and eternal God, to be the Creator, Upholder, and Ruler of the world; and that hold themselves obliged in conscience to live peaceably and justly in civil society, shall in no ways, be molested or prejudiced for their religious persuasion, or practice, in matters of faith and worship, nor shall they be compelled, at any time, to frequent or maintain any religious worship, place or ministry whatsoever.

Pennsylvania's religious liberty made it "an asylum for banished sects," a place of unprecedented pluralism. This was no accident, for Quaker missionaries, including Penn himself, went to Europe to court like-minded religious groups, who were pariahs in their own countries. Europeans, especially German-speaking groups, responded. As early as 1683, Mennonites arrived in Pennsylvania, to be followed shortly by Dunkers, Schwenkfelders, and other sects heretofore unknown in North America. Rosicrucians appeared and lived in caves along the banks of the Wissahickon Creek, awaiting the "Woman of the Wilderness," whose arrival would usher in the millennium. A group of German Baptists arrived, who were accused of attempting to revive Judaism by refusing to eat pork and circumcizing each other "after the Jewish manner." Every ship docking in Philadelphia seemed to disgorge some new sect or utopian group.

Penn and his contemporary, Roger Williams, both founded colonies offering unrestricted religious liberty, grounded in the New Testament and on the promise of economic prosperity. Why has posterity treated them so differently? Why at the time of the American Revolution was Williams a virtual nonperson and Penn a celebrity? What had Penn done to be saluted by Thomas Jefferson as the "greatest law-giver the world has produced" and by John Adams as a person "worthy of eternal remembrance," despite his "raging appetite for land?"

What Penn had done was to establish and set in motion a colony that by 1776 was an economic powerhouse, its wealth and population booming, its capital the second largest city in the British Empire, its politics stable (except for the eruption of frontier fury in 1764). Pennsylvania was a standing refutation of the old Elizabethan fears that religious pluralism led to social chaos and irrefutable evidence that religious liberty, as Penn had predicted, would foster economic prosperity. From 1774 onward, advocates of unfettered freedom of religion in the new American nation cited Pennsylvania as proof that religious liberty was morally right and politically and economically beneficial. In 1774 James Madison wrote a college friend that Pennsylvanians had "long felt the good effects of their religious as well as Civil Liberty. Foreigners have been encouraged to settle among you. Industry and Virtue have been promoted. . . . Commerce and art have flourished and I can not help attributing those continual exertions of Genius which appear among you to the inspiration of Liberty." "Our sister states of Pennsylvania and New Jersey," wrote Thomas Jefferson in 1781, "have long subsisted without any establishment at all. The experiment was new and doubtful when they made it. It has answered beyond conception. They flourish infinitely. Religion is well supported; of various kinds, indeed, but all good enough. All sufficient to preserve peace and order . . . their harmony is unparalleled." Farther to the south, William Tennent delivered a speech to the South Carolina General Assembly in 1777 in which he attacked "religious establishments. "Every fetter," claimed Tennent,

> whether religious or civil, deters people from settling in a new country . . . an entire equality has made Pennsylvania the emporeum of America to the immortal honor of its wise legislator; what good effects may not be expected from the same spirit of laws in this country? That state in America which adopts the freest and most liberal plan will be the most opulent and powerful and will well deserve it.

William Penn, the "wise legislator," was admired in new United States by those Americans who shared his views on religious liberty. They believed that he had seen the future and knew that it would work.

One more colony, New Hampshire, was established during the years between the Restoration of Charles II and the Glorious Revolution. It can be considered a would-be proprietorship. Englishmen fishermen and Indian traders settled in New Hampshire as early as 1624, and thereafter the territory received a steady stream of settlers from Massachusetts, its southern neighbor. A group of promoters, organized in 1620 as the Council for New England, granted land patents for chunks of New Hampshire to some of their colleagues. These worthies were soon parties to disputes with the government of Massachusetts, which asserted conflicting land claims and which commanded the allegiance of the towns in southern New Hampshire. These towns followed the Massachusetts model of establishing a Congregational church from which no dissent was permitted. In the 1650s Quakers were expelled from New Hampshire by being dragged behind a cart and whipped from town to town. Anglicans complained that they were not permitted "common prayer sacraments." Persecution was absent, however, in the largest town, Portsmouth, where Anglicans and Congregationalists worshiped in "peaceful co-existence."

In the 1670s a grandson of one of the original New Hampshire patentees, Robert Tufton Mason, enlisted powerful allies to lobby royal authorities for the creation of a proprietorship in New Hampshire similar to those of Carolina and New Jersey. Mason, however, failed to generate sufficient influence to sway Charles II's advisors, who, instead, in 1679, made New Hampshire a royal colony. Consistent with the post-Restoration policy of the British government to support religious liberty in the North American colonies, the first royal governor of New Hampshire was instructed that "we do hereby require and command that liberty of conscience shall be allowed unto all protestants; that such especially as shall be conformable to the rites of the Church of England shall be particularly countenanced and encouraged." What this last phrase meant was uncertain. Did it anticipate, as similar language in the proprietary charters of North

Carolina and New Jersey appeared to do, future and potentially heavy-handed state intervention in the colony's religious sphere?

In 1666 a certain George Alsop described the condition of religion in Maryland as "the Miracle of this Age." This observation was applicable to the religious situation in the seventeenth-century North American colonies collectively. It did, in fact, seem close to miraculous that Catholics and Quakers, whose religions were hated and persecuted in England, governed major colonies in North America. And was it any less wondrous that, in the years immediately following the restoration of Charles II in 1660, liberty of conscience was officially sanctioned in the North American colonies at the very time the English Parliament was enacting the Clarendon Code, a ruthless attempt to impose religious uniformity in the mother country?

One reason for the disconnect between religious policy in England and her colonies was what might be called a "no peace beyond the line" mentality, an attitude among English officials borrowed from a contemporary geopolitical convention that held that west of the longitude of the Azores the rules of European statecraft did not apply and that any kind of unconventional policy could be initiated with impunity. The Carolina charter of 1665 disclosed this mentality by excusing its generous grant of liberty of conscience on the grounds that "the remote distance" of the new colony would preclude any adverse impact in England.

The anything goes attitudes of English royal officials produced the crazy quilt pattern of state–church relations in the North American colonies. There were colonies – Virginia, Massachusetts, and Connecticut – in which the state enforced religious uniformity with the vigor of the medieval, Hildebrandine Catholic Church. In other colonies – Pennsylvania, West New Jersey, and Rhode Island – exactly the opposite policy prevailed, the state being divested of power in the religious sphere. Between these two poles were three colonies – Maryland, Carolina, and East New Jersey – where religious freedom existed against the background of a prospective state establishment. In New York the government had the option of supporting multiple religions with toleration for dissenters; in New Hampshire government enforced conformity on the Massachusetts model in some places but not in others.

Where religious liberty existed in the colonies, a robust pluralism prevailed, so robust that only the religious landscape in the Netherlands could be compared to it. In this respect the religious environment in the majority of the colonies truly was one of the miracles of the age. By the time of the Glorious Revolution of 1688 pluralism, where it existed in America, was so firmly entrenched that any attempt to impose religious uniformity would have been futile.

Liberty of conscience, written into so many charters drafted after the outbreak of the English civil wars and especially after the Restoration, sounds very modern but, in fact, it had a much narrower meaning in seventeenth-century America than it has in the first decade of the 21st century. In many documents liberty and state power coexisted. Maryland's Act Concering Religion (1649) promised "free exercise" of religion, the exact words of the First Amendment to the U.S. Constitution, and at the same time authorized the state to hang non-Trinitarian Christians. In instructions of April 23, 1664, to investigators heading to Massachusetts, Charles II's government inserted an article on "liberty of conscience," the "observation and preservation" of which was declared to be "our very hearty purpose and determination." Liberty of conscience was evidently assumed to be compatible with the suffocating state control of religion in the Bay Colony, for the commissioners were instructed to assure the Puritans that there was not "any purpose in us to . . . introduce any other forme of worshipp among them than what they have chosen." The various Carolina charters guaranteed "Liberty of Conscience," even as the Church of England was designated as the "only and Orthodox, and the National Religion" of the colony, entitled to receive tax support. The New Jersey Charter of 1665 proclaimed "Liberty of Conscience" and permitted the General Assembly to tax the citizens for the "maintenance" of the clergy. In 1669 a New Yorker wrote a correspondent in England that the colony offered "Liberty of Conscience to all, provided they raise not fundamentalls in religion," by which he presumably meant that the state could suppress heterodox opinions and not compromise religious liberty. Consider England itself. In March 1672 Charles II issued his famous Declaration of Indulgence (retracted the next year) in which he "suspended all manner of penal laws in matters ecclesiastical." Dissenters could now worship without molestation, if they bought licenses from royal authorities. But they must continue paying tithes to the Church of England and suffering disqualification from public offices on religious grounds. Nevertheless, London's dissenting ministers appeared before Charles II on March 28, 1672, and praised him for granting "the liberty of our consciences." Liberty of conscience in seventeenth century England and her colonies was in no way incompatible with the exercise of strong and, if necessary, punitive state power.

What the seventeenth century people of England and settlers of America wanted, when they claimed liberty of conscience, was what Sir Isaiah Berlin has called "negative liberty," which meant being left alone as they went about their spiritual business. The seventeenth-century charters repeatedly assured the settlers that they would, in fact, be left alone and not "be any ways molested, punished, disquieted, or called in question" for their "opinion or practice in matters of religious Concernment."

Public practice of religion was the key demand of dissenters. "The doctrine set forth by the Elizabethan Settlement was," in the words of an expert, that "the conscience was free although the public exercise of any but the established religion was not to be tolerated." By the middle of the seventeenth-century, this doctrine was described by Anglican authorities and major thinkers like Hobbes and Locke in the language of the ancient theological construct, *adiaphora* – a term that meant things indifferent in religion. External manifestations of religion, in contrast to "Internall Faith" (Hobbes's term), were considered to be matters of indifference, not essential to salvation, which could, therefore, be regulated or suppressed by the magistrate. Before he changed his mind in 1667, Locke distinguished between "mental states like belief or assent," which could not be controlled by the state, and "outward actions," which could be because they were not essential for salvation. Dissenters rejected this distinction and argued that "conscience could not be free without freedom of action," that "liberty of conscience was not a mere freedom to believe 'but the exercise of ourselves in a visible way of worship.'" To be unmolested in a public, "visible way of worship" was what the seventeenth-century dissenters craved, in exchange for which they were prepared to acquiesce in intrusive state action in many sectors of the religious sphere.

For the seventeenth century, liberty of conscience was unmolested public worship, which liberated dissenters from what they described as "fear, distress, and distracting anxieties, and trials in their persons (rendering their lives burthensome to themselves and useless to others.)" It fell far short of the modern definition of liberty of conscience as an illimitable entitlement, wrapped in the mantle of a right, trumping the power of the state. This modern definition was scarcely conceivable at the time of the Glorious Revolution of 1688. By 1776 it had secured beach heads in some parts of America, but as late as 1789 it was resisted by substantial numbers of congressmen who drafted the federal Bill of Rights.

2

To the American Revolution

HE GLORIOUS REVOLUTION OF 1688 OCCURRED WHEN
the Dutch Protestant prince, William of Orange, invaded
England in November of that year and, without bloodshed, overthrew the Catholic king, James II. The revolution had a momentous
effect on both the theory and practice of church–state relations in
England and, derivatively, in North America.

The authoritarian policies of James II, which led to his demise in
England, were nowhere more conspicuous than in his administration
of the North American colonies. When James ascended the throne in
1685, he and his advisers were confronted in North America with a
potpourri of colonies whose political and economic conditions were
at least as diverse as their religious systems. Weak and insubor-
dinate, they could not defend themselves nor would they enforce
English trade regulations. James decided to abolish the proprietary
and charter colonies, to consolidate them into two jurisdictions,
divided by a line running east to west from a point just north of
Philadelphia and to govern them with royal proconsuls.

The success of James's plan, which looked good on paper to
imperial bureaucrats, depended on the sensitivity with which it
was implemented in the colonies. In 1686 a Dominion of New
England was created (eventually containing New York and New

Jersey), administration of which was delegated to a military martinet, Sir Edmund Andros. Continuing the English government's religious policy in the colonies, James directed that liberty of conscience prevail in the Dominion. The imperious Andros forced Boston's Old South Congregational Church to share its facilities with a Church of England minister, for which action he and his advisers were denounced as "bloody Devotees of Rome" who intended the "Extinction of the Protestant Religion." Andros further infuriated Massachusetts by challenging the validity of the colonists' land titles and by governing without a representative assembly.

When news arrived in Boston in April 1689 that James had been expelled from England, Massachusetts staged its own revolution by capturing and imprisoning Andros and his cronies and reestablishing popular government. Another armed rebellion swept Dominion officials out of New York. In Maryland Lord Baltimore's government was forcibly replaced by "an association in arms for the defense of the Protestant religion." Those colonies whose charters had been revoked returned to the old ways, pending the receipt of information about the new king's policies.

William took his time in formulating a colonial policy, waiting until the fall of 1691, for example, to give Massachusetts a new government. In the meantime, in 1689, the King and Parliament tackled the religious issues raised by the revolution by passing the Toleration Act, the most important reform of England's religious life since Henry VIII's break with the Church of Rome in the 1530s, more significant even than the measures enacted from 1642 to 1660, since the Toleration Act enjoyed broader public support and endured well into the nineteenth century.

The Toleration Act took the same approach as Charles II's short-lived Declaration of Indulgence by exempting dissenters from the

Church of England from penalties imposed upon them by the nation's ecclesiastical laws. Unlike Charles II's declaration, the Toleration Act applied to orthodox protestant dissenters only; Catholics and anti-Trinitarians were excluded from its benefits. The act relieved orthodox dissenters in two ways: (1) dissenting ministers could function without interference if they took the oaths of allegiance and supremacy before a justice of the peace in open court and subscribed to what was commonly called the Test or the "declaration against Popery," a statement repudiating the doctrine of transubstantiation and thus disqualifying Catholics; in addition, ministers were required to subscribe to the Thirty-Nine Articles of the Church of England, modified to permit Presbyterians, Independents, Baptists, and Quakers to consent in good conscience; and (2) dissenting meetinghouses were eligible for use, if they were registered in a civil or ecclesiastical court and if services were conducted with doors open.

Questions about the meaning and intent of the Toleration Act were raised as soon as its terms became public. In both England and North America, for example, there were questions about the act's scope: Did it apply only to "settled" ministers or were itinerant preachers also covered? Americans argued about a more fundamental issue: Was the act valid in the colonies? By 1710 Tories and Whigs in England had developed competing theories about the scope of the act, which were angrily aired at the Sacheverell trial. As late as the 1760s, the meaning of the act was disputed by two giants of the law, Lord Mansfield and Sir William Blackstone.

About one point there was no dispute: the Toleration Act was remarkably successful in mobilizing the dissenters to take advantage of their new status; between 1689 and 1710 they established no fewer than 3,901 places of public worship. The Church of England was, of course, distressed at these inroads on its membership. Scholars estimate that during the reign of Queen Anne (1702–1714) as many as 80 percent of Anglican clergymen opposed the Toleration Act and demanded its repeal or modification. During this period High Church mobs "rabbl'd, pulled down and burnt" dissenting meeting houses. Bishop Burnet lamented that so large a number of Churchmen were filled with the "mad rage of zealots."

Though less demonstrative than Queen Anne's infuriated Church-men, twentieth-century scholars have also been offended by the Toleration Act, for today the idea of religious toleration is scorned – an "insult to mankind" in the words of Justice Oliver Wendell Holmes. Modern scholars have, consequently, been unrestrained in denouncing the Toleration Act as "freakish," "most unsatisfactory," "one of the worst forms of tyranny." A scholar, who in the 1930s wrote three authoritative volumes on religious toleration in Tudor–Stuart England, assured his readers that "toleration . . . falls considerably short of religious liberty," a judgment that would have dumbfounded the seventeenth- and eighteenth-century beneficiaries of the Toleration Act, who were profuse in public expressions of gratitude, elated that the statute had granted them liberty of conscience and something dearer: the "natural right" to religious liberty.

This the dissenters believed despite the government's imposition upon them of numerous burdens because of their religious noncon-formity. Besides requiring dissenters to jump through the hoops of registering, swearing, and subscribing in court, the Toleration Act explicitly permitted the state to tax them for the support of the Church of England and to try them in ecclesiastical courts for noncompli-ance. The act left standing the Corporation Act of 1661 and the Test Act of 1673, which barred dissenters from public office unless they took communion according to the rites of the Church of England.

And it did not disturb statutes that prevented dissenters from receiving a university education unless they subscribed to articles of the Church of England.

It is instructive to sample contemporary comments on the Toleration Act, so reviled in the twentieth century. In 1702, Daniel Defoe, a Baptist, urged his brethren "annually to commemorate, by a standing law among themselves, that great day of their deliverance, when it pleased God to tread down persecution, oppression, church-tyranny and state-tyranny under the feet of the law and to establish the liberty of their consciences, which they had long prayed for, in a public and legal toleration." In 1732, Daniel Neal, an Independent minister, famous for his *History of the Puritans*, urged his coreligionists to be grateful for the Toleration Act, which had delivered them from the "Yoke of Oppression" and made them "Secure of their Civil and Religious Liberties." A few years later a major Anglican thinker praised "the divine doctrine of toleration, or the right of worshiping God according to one's own conscience." In 1759, Richard Price, a Presbyterian minister considered an oracle of freedom by many of the Founding Fathers, asserted that "our religious liberty," secured by the Toleration Act, "is the crown of all our advantages. There are other nations, who enjoy civil and religious liberty as well as we, though perhaps not so completely. But with respect to religious liberty we are almost singular and unparalleled." In 1771 Philip Furneaux, a dissenting minister and, according to John Adams, a favorite of Thomas Jefferson, in his *Letters to the Honourable Mr. Justice Blackstone*, saluted "that great prince, King William, to whom the Dissenters are, under God, alone obliged for their deliverance from unjust violence and oppression; and for being restored, in part, to their natural rights by toleration. I say, to their natural rights: for religious liberty is one of those rights to which men are entitled by nature." The next year, John Wesley, the founder of the Methodist Church, asked: "What is the Liberty which we want? It is not Civil or Religious Liberty. These we have in such a degree that was never known before, not from the times of William the Conqueror."

These tributes to "singular and unparalleled" religious liberty bestowed by the Toleration Act were made at progressively later dates during the eighteenth century when the laws requiring dissenters to swear special oaths, taxing them for the support of the Church of England, "incapacitating" them from public office, and depriving them of a university education on religious grounds remained in full force. The dissenters tried unsuccessfully in the 1730s to obtain the repeal of the Test and Corporation Acts, but their failure to do so in no way altered their view that the disabilities under which they suffered had no adverse impact on their liberty of conscience, defined as unimpeded public worship.

This message reached America through the writings of the influential authors just quoted and through others who had an audience in the colonies, but it obtained its widest publicity as the result of a decision rendered on August 16, 1732, by the King's attorney and solicitor generals, Yorke and Talbot, on a petition brought by the Society for the Propagation of the Gospel against the government of Massachusetts, protesting the Bay Colony's taxation of members of the Church of England to support the Congregational Church. This case was a cause celebre in Anglican circles and, though actively supported by the Bishop of London and other highly placed members of the Anglican hierarchy, it simmered for six years before the King's highest law officers ruled against the Anglicans, holding that the authority of a state to regulate religion was broad enough to authorize the taxation of members of the official church of the Empire for the benefit of dissenters, without offending against the fundamental principle of religious freedom. The law officers of the crown wrote that the Massachusetts legislators "may take care and provide for the Celebration of the Publick Worship of God, and for the Maintenance of Ministers as incident thereto, and doing of this in a reasonable manner cannot be said to be inconsistent with Liberty of Conscience."

The assumption that the state's coercive power in religious affairs and liberty of conscience were compatible was a feature of several colonial charters, issued after the restoration of Charles II. The Toleration Act, therefore, broke no fresh ground by embodying this view. What was new, in fact, what was revolutionary about the Toleration Act, was that it shattered the principal rationale for state support of religion that had existed since the Roman Empire. According to the traditional theory, one religion had a monopoly of the truth and the state, which "had the care of souls," was obliged to impose that truth on the body politic lest it be deprived of the opportunity to gain eternal salvation. The Toleration Act proclaimed that there was no longer a monopoly of religious truth in England that the state was obliged to promote. It permitted four denominations – Presbyterians, Independents, Baptists, and Quakers – to dispense their own versions of the truth in competition with the Church of England. Or, to state the reverse, the Toleration Act permitted four religions to propagate with impunity what the Church of England had previously considered as lethal theological errors. It created a free market in religious truth in which the British consumer, not the state, decided what would be in his or her best interest.

If the state was no longer in the business of promoting theological truth, why after the passage of the Toleration Act did it continue to give preferential support to the Church of England clergymen in the form of "maintenance" – salaries generated by taxes on the

entire population? In earlier days material support for ministers
had been an afterthought. Calvin had acknowledged that the state
should "supply the pastors and ministers of the Word with all that
is necessary for food and maintenance" but he insisted that the
magistrate's primary duty was to "bravely defend the doctrine of
the Word," which contained the saving truth. No one doubted that
paying ministers was covered by Isaiah's scriptural mandate that
magistrates be nursing fathers of the church. Some, in fact, thought
this metaphor made it particularly appropriate that the state provide
the ministers' financial sustenance, for then the clergy would "suck
the breasts of kings (earthly things are the milk of kingly breasts.)"
But even if there were a scriptural warrant for the practice, what
was the payoff for a salaried clergy, no longer armed by the state to
impose truth?

William Warburton, later Bishop of Gloucester, supplied the
answer in 1736 in his classic volume, the *Alliance between Church
and State*. In capital letters Warburton asserted that "THE TRUE
END FOR WHICH RELIGION IS ESTABLISHED IS NOT TO PROVIDE
FOR THE TRUE FAITH, BUT FOR CIVIL UTILITY." Like most of
Warburton's opinions, this conclusion was far from original – Plato
and Aristotle had preached the social utility of religion. In 1735
a pamphleteer had expressed what had become a cliche among
the British intelligentsia, that the state's support of the Church of
England must be justified "not by the truth of anglican doctrine but
by the value of religion to civil government." But Warburton's book
was written with such forceful clarity and abundance of documentation that a twentieth-century authority, Harold Laski, hailed it as
the "one volume upon the problem of church and state," written
in eighteenth-century England, that "deserves more than passing
notice." Warburton redefined the church's primary mission as being

service to the state not the salvation of souls. "The Church," he said, "should serve the State and the State protect the Church." And how should the church serve the state? By creating, Warburton answered, what politicians today would call law and order.

What was there about religion that enabled it to promote the essence of "civil utility," a law-abiding, peaceful kingdom? From Elizabethan times to the Glorious Revolution, uniformity of religion, imposed by the state, was assumed to be a prerequisite for this goal. The Toleration Act undermined this assumption by producing diversity of religion. Yet Warburton argued that religion had lost none of its capacity to produce stability. How could it deliver the same results – peace and order – under the new conditions? Warburton supplied the answer in a companion volume to the *Alliance*, the *Divine Legation of Moses Demonstrated* (1737), which was even more popular than his earlier book. Once again using capital letters, Warburton proclaimed that "THE DOCTRINE OF A FUTURE STATE OF REWARDS AND PUNISHMENTS, IS NECESSARY TO THE WELL BEING OF CIVIL SOCIETY." What Warburton meant was that the fear of eternal punishment, preached by religions both orthodox and heterodox in the most lurid manner, produced law and order by frightening the common man, especially the "vulgar," into peaceful, law-abiding behavior. Religion, wrote Warburton, was "the great Bridle of the Multitude, to whose Passions" it was "obliged to speak," for it "could never pretend to govern them by Reason or Philosophy."

Again, there was nothing original about Warburton's conclusions. According to a contemporary, Viscount Bolingbroke, the future state doctrine "began to be taught long before we have any light into antiquity, and when we begin to have any, we find it established." Since the civil war of the 1640s "governing conduct" had been a subject that preoccupied some of Britain's best minds. Thinkers debated the best way to create a peaceful, well-behaved population, which would bring stability to England, a nation that, in J. H. Plumb's words, "for centuries . . . had scarcely been free from turbulence for more than a decade at a time." Thomas Hobbes was convinced that only an absolute government could maintain order over time, but most of his contemporaries thought that producing orderly subjects was preferable to submitting to a leviathan state. To these thinkers employing the doctrine of a future state of rewards and punishment, which meant relying on religion, was the best path to stability. In 1966 Jacob Viner asserted that the future state doctrine, which he called the "providential apparatus," was "one of the great governing mechanism of the early modern European church and state. The practice associated with it was attrition: the fear of divine punishment (hell) and the hope of divine reward (heaven) are necessary to motivate people to act in accordance with moral and legal systems." All but a few theorists, Viner continued, "held that a belief in providentialism must underlie any stable social order."

Locke formulated his own version of the future state doctrine, which a scholar has called "penalism." The doctrine was so pervasive in the eighteenth century that, according to Swift's hero, Lemuel Gulliver, British horses were familiar with it. Even sceptics patronized the doctrine. In *The Decline and Fall*, Gibbon recommend that magistrates support the future state doctrine even if they believed it to be false. "Whatever you decide in your own mind," an advocate of Gibbon's position wrote, "the received doctrine and words must be used for the people" who are "inclined to vice and can be deterred from evil only by the fear of punishment."

That one of religion's roles was to produce social stability and that the state supported it to achieve that result was an ancient assumption. The idea that the state's *primary* purpose in supporting religion was to produce social stability – that the promotion of salvation through truth was relegated to, at best, a back burner – was a radical reconceptualization of the theory of church and state, produced by the passage of the Toleration Act of 1689 and by the efforts of British thinkers – Warburton and others – to make sense of the meaning of the statute.

By 1750 most informed Britons had come to the following conclusions about the relationship of state to church. They believed that government's support of religion was a timeless practice. They believed that there was unassailable scriptural authority, preeminently the nursing fathers passage in Isaiah 49:23, to justify the practice. They believed that the state's powers in the religious realm were broad – broad enough to include discrimination against minorities – but were still in "perfect Concord and Agreement" with religious liberty. And they believed that these powers, when exercised, brought indispensable benefits to the state and to society. By 1750 many in the American colonies shared these views, especially in those colonies where there were established churches.

The Glorious Revolution more than doubled the number of established churches in the American colonies. The revolution ignited a movement that historians have called Anglicization, whose principal feature was a desire by colonists and English officials to make American life and institutions more like English ones. This impulse operated across the board in America, extending from architecture to law to religion and worked in favor of the Church of England, an icon of life in the mother country. The revolution, which sealed the victory of the Church over the "Catholic menace" represented by James II, invigorated its leaders and their political allies to secure the Church's ascendancy throughout the Empire. Queen Anne (1702–1714), a self-proclaimed champion of the Church, was an potent ally.

One of the most conspicuous fruits of Anglicization in the colonies was the installation of royal governments in the proprietary colonies. It was assumed that royal government required the establishment of the Church of England. "You are big," the new royal governor of New York, Benjamin Fletcher, lectured his legislature in 1692, "with the privileges of Englishmen and Magna Charta, which is your right; and the same law, doth provide for the Religion of the Church of England." Using Warburton's rationale, British officials supported strengthening the Church in the colonies for political reasons; a more energetic church was expected to create peaceful, law-abiding citizens, who would not disturb the colonial regimes. "In respect to the colonies," wrote a British official, "it is evident, I think, beyond contradiction, that to secure their obedience no way can be so effectual as a regular establishment of the Church of England, with resident bishops."

Maryland was the first proprietary colony to establish a royal government in the wake of the Glorious Revolution. The Protestant forces who overthrew Lord Baltimore in 1689 hoped that a royal government and an established Church of England would once and for all suppress their Catholic rivals. The Protestants were led by John Coode, a renegade Anglican priest, given to "excessive drinking, blasphemous lewd talking and swearing." At an assembly convened by the first royal governor, Sir Lionel Copley, in the spring of 1692, Coode and his followers passed an act establishing the Church of England and taxing the adherents of others religions to support it. This act, which appeared to criminalize the practice of all other religions in the colony, was the first of several similar bills rejected in England despite the efforts to confirm them by two notable figures in the history of religion in the American colonies, Francis Nicholson and Thomas Bray.

Nicholson was a roving royal governor, serving in five colonies, stretching from Nova Scotia to South Carolina between 1689 and the 1720s. He served in Maryland between 1694 to 1698. His generosity to the Church of England was legendary. He donated an estimated £2,000 to the Church during his lifetime, a huge sum which earned him the accolade of "nursing father of our holy Mother" Church of England. At a convention of Anglican clergymen in 1713 Nicholson was compared favorably to Queen Anne, "who has always proved herself a Nursing Mother to the Church." Nicholson, however, was anything but nurturing to his fellow citizens. He was so frequently consumed by "excessive fits of passion" that a contemporary claimed that he was "born drunk." He regularly berated and assaulted his associates. He treated the colonists with unbounded contempt, threatening to "hang them with Magna Charta [which he called Magna Farta] about their necks." He was also a womanizer. A disgusted acquaintance denounced him as "a monstrous compound of hypocrisy and profaneness." Nicholson's esteem for the Church of England obviously did not translate into personal piety. The reason, as a student of his career has observed, was that Nicholson's supported the Church solely as an instrument to instill "political obedience." He could have cared less, apparently, about the Church as a source of Christian morality. Nicholson's view of the church as primarily a partner of the state in producing civil utility appears to have been shared by some Anglican clergymen, especially in the southern colonies, and may have contributed to those examples of morally corrupt and irresponsible personal behavior for which the clergy as a whole was frequently, and, as recent scholarship has demonstrated, unfairly condemned.

Thomas Bray arrived in Maryland in 1699, just as Nicholson left. He appeared as a deputy (commissary) of the Bishop of London, who exercised jurisdiction over the colonial Church. Bray's task was to supervise the Maryland clergy, only five of whom were officiating in the colony in 1692, too few to prevent Maryland from becoming what an Anglican priest, a few years earlier, described as a "Sodom of uncleanness & a Pest house of Iniquity." Bray returned the next year to England, where he assisted in establishing the Society for the Propagation of the Gospel in Foreign Parts, an organization dedicated to supplying Anglican missionaries to America and other parts of the Empire, where the Church of England was underserved. The S.P G., as it was called, sent as many 600 ministers to North America in the eighteenth century who spurred the growth of the Church, but it ignited controversy and suspicion by sending missionaries to New England, which was fully staffed with Congregational clergymen.

Of more local interest was Bray's efforts to obtain royal confirmation of a Maryland act of 1700 which established the Church of England in the colony. The problem with the 1700 act, as with every other church establishment act passed in Maryland since 1692, was that it appeared to require all religious groups in the colony to conform to the Church of England. The Board of Trade, adhering to the fixed official policy mandating liberty of conscience in the colony, rejected the bill but promised to approved a new one "with proper alterations agreeable to the toleration allowed here." Bray drafted several bills before he crafted acceptable language. His bill, approved at length by the Board of Trade, was sent to Maryland where the assembly passed it on March 16, 1702. It became the foundation document for church–state relations for the remainder of the colonial period.

The "Act for the Establishment of Religious Worship, according to the Church of England" explicitly applied to Maryland the English Toleration Act of 1689, thus granting the people of Maryland liberty of conscience as it was understood at the time. The act also relieved Maryland Quakers by granting them the benefit of an English act of 1696, excusing them from the obligation to take oaths. On the other hand, the act of 1702 required everyone in the colony to pay taxes to support the Church of England, making a citizen who before the Revolution had, in the absence of state control, enjoyed religious equality with his Anglican neighbor a tributary to the neighbor's church. The establishment of the Church of England in Maryland did not diminish the robust religious pluralism in the province, noted in 1666, but it put an end to the religious equality that prevailed in the seventeenth century. And this, of course, created widespread resentment.

A campaign to establish the Church of England in North and South Carolina followed closely on the heels of the effort in Maryland. North Carolina Anglicans sought to disfranchise Quakers and South Carolina Anglicans, known as the Goose Creek men, aimed to eliminate the influence of sectaran opponents, who opposed their program for defense against the Spanish and for regulation of the Indian trade. A critic accused the Goose Creek men of turning "the civil differences in Carolina into a religious controversy." The South Carolina campaign was instigated by zealous Church of England men, who like other Anglicans, had been invigorated by the Church's improved fortunes after the Glorious Revolution. Foremost among these was the principal proprietor of the province, Lord John Granville, "an inflexible bigot for the High Church," and his lieutenants in South Carolina, Governor Nathaniel Johnson and Chief Justice Nicholas Trott, both also accused of Anglican bigotry. In 1704 Johnson rammed an exclusion act, incapacitating anyone from public service who did not take communion according to the rites of the Church of England, through an illegally constituted assembly by one vote. This act extended to South Carolina the English Test and Corporation Acts, which disqualified dissenters in the mother country from public office. The preface to the South Carolina exclusion act claimed that its intention was not "persecutions for conscience," thus reflecting the post-Toleration Act view that discriminatory religious legislation was not incompatible with liberty of conscience. Along with the exclusion act, the South Carolina legislature passed an act establishing the Church of England, funding its ministers from tax revenues.

Opponents sent agents to London to demand the repeal of these laws and hired Daniel Defoe to conduct a public relations campaign against the proprietor and his local minions. Their efforts were successful. As they had in Maryland, British officials intervened on behalf of liberty of conscience in South Carolina. In 1706 the House of Lords addressed Queen Anne, denouncing the Exclusion Act as "repugnant to the Laws of England" and, worse, "destructive to trade" and tending to the "depopulating and ruining of the province." The Privy Council commanded the proprietors to reject the exclusion and establishment laws and began exploring ways to vacate their charter, initiating a process that culminated in the antiproprietary rebellion in South Carolina in 1719 and the establishment of royal government. The revolt, a scholar has asserted, was "an expression of the Carolinians' desire to make themselves as much like Englishmen as possible, and royal government was obviously a step in that direction." As a result of the royal rebuke to Governor Johnson and the Goose Creek men, the South Carolina Assembly in 1706 repealed the exclusion act and passed a "Church Act," which regulated church–state relations for the remainder of the colonial period. The Church Act established the Church of England and laid taxes to support it. To soften the blow to dissenters, who were now officially tolerated, the assembly resolved to support the Church of England from general revenues – taxes on exports and, later, imports – which eliminated the abrasive personal encounters with sheriffs and other local functionaries who dunned dissenters for church taxes in other colonies. According to an eighteenth-century Baptist historian, the assembly offered to let dissenters share the tax receipts, which they declined. The proprietors also attempted to lower the temperature in the colony by appointing a new governor who was instructed to "show the greatest Tenderness" to dissenters.

The Church Act did not discourage dissenters from coming to South Carolina. After 1720 they began pouring into the colony from Northern Ireland, Germany and other parts of America in such numbers that Francis Nicholson, who was appointed governor in 1720, predicted in 1724 that they might "soon overrun the colony," a refrain that was repeatedly heard in later years. Said another Anglican: "if more Church of England ministers don't come, the province will be inundated by German, French, and Irish, and the interests of the Church, will be entirely lost, for they are already at a very low Ebb." The Church Act of 1706 put South Carolina in the same situation as Maryland after the passage of its 1702 establishment act: pronounced pluralism, liberty of conscience for dissenters in a tolerated status and a loss of equality between the Church of England and all other competing denominations, "a circumstance that did not fail to rankle in the hearts of dissenters in the colony for two or three generations."

A parallel effort was mounted to establish the Church of England in North Carolina, which was not officially separated, as a royal government, from South Carolina until 1729. The Quakers were strong in North Carolina, where no less a person than George Fox had preached in 1672. In 1694, a Quaker, John Archdale, was appointed governor. The first Church of England minister in the colony's history, Daniel Brett, arrived in 1700. According to a "zealous Churchman," Brett behaved "in a most horrid manner [and] broke out in such an extravagant course that I am ashamed to express his carriage." In 1702 the Anglican partisan, Sir Nathaniel Johnson, was appointed governor of both South and North Carolina. Johnson appointed as his deputy in North Carolina, Colonel Robert Daniel, a "cruel and merciless" man, who had "great zeal for the Established Church." In 1704 Daniel contrived to have the North Carolina Assembly pass by "one or two" votes a "Vestry Act" which sought to obtain precisely the same objective as the South Carolina acts of 1704: exclusion of dissenters from the political process and establishment of the Church of England. Since no copies of this or a church act passed the next year have survived, it is impossible to tell how oppressive they were, but they were offensive enough to non-Anglicans to throw the colony into turmoil, which led to a brief civil war – Cary's rebellion – in 1711. After the rebellion was quelled, another attempt was made to establish the Church of England and yet another in 1715, which finally established the church and "granted indulgences to Protestant dissenters," presumably those that they enjoyed under the Toleration Act of 1689.

The acts passed on the Church's behalf did her little good. The few Anglican priests who ventured into North Carolina found the land full of poverty and contentious dissenters, who controlled vestries and refused to pay a living wage. One frustrated Anglican minister declared that he would "rather be a curate of a Bear Garden than Bishop of Carolina." Years passed without the presence of any Church of England ministers in North Carolina, even as dissenters of various denominations thrived. The Church was, in fact, established on paper only. An Anglican minister complained in 1743 that "No province in America...has more need of Missionaries and none can deserve them less." Some years later the religious condition of the "poor and unhappy" province of North Carolina looked so grim to a Baptist observer that he compared it to "Israel in the time of Isaiah. 'From the sole of the foot to the crown of the head, without any soundness, but wounds and bruises and putrifying sores.'"

In 1702 East and West New Jersey were consolidated into a single royal colony. In deference, apparently, to the overwhelming Quaker presence in West Jersey, English officials did not attempt to establish the Church of England in the colony. A curious feature of the new royal government in New Jersey was that, until 1738, the governor of New York was its chief executive.

Church–state issues created turbulence in New York "The missionary zeal appearing in the English church" after the Glorious Revolution made itself felt there in 1692 in the person of Governor Benjamin Fletcher, who appeared with instructions to establish the Church of England. "Convinced of the superiority of the dogmas and organization of the English state church," Fletcher matched the zeal of Francis Nicholson in Maryland and Richard Johnson in South Carolina in attempting to fulfill his instructions. Fletcher's task was no easier than theirs because the Church of England was as weak in New York as it was in the other two provinces; as late as 1704 there were only four Anglican ministers in the colony, serving just two churches. In 1693 Fletcher pressured the New York Assembly, controlled by dissenters, into passing an act, entitled "An Act for Settling a Ministry & Raising a Maintenance for them." The act, which applied only to the city and county of New York, and to the counties of Richmond, Queens and Westchester, did not mention the Church of England and meant, the assembly contended, that a "Dissenting Protestant Minister" could be elected by the vestries in those counties and, as the established minister, receive tax support. Fletcher and his allies rejected this interpretation, and with the help of the Dutch Reformed.Church, whom the governor rewarded with an improvised legal establishment of its own, Fletcher succeeded in establishing, at least to his own satisfaction, the Church of England in New York City and the counties immediately surrounding it, although not at the expense of the dissenters' liberty of conscience. Dissenters never accepted that the Church of England was legally established by the act of 1693.

In 1699 Fletcher's successor, the Earl of Bellomont, signed a law permitting the counties outside New York City and its environs to continue, in a modified way, the practice sanctioned by the Duke's Laws of 1665, allowing tax money to be appropriated to the church of the majority of citizens of individual towns, creating conditions in some towns where Presbyterians "stick not to call themselves the Established Church & us [Anglicans] Dissenters." The different kinds of church establishments in New York have prompted historians to complain about the "imprecise" and "confusing" nature of church–state relations in the colony. What is clear is that the citizens of the colony did not object to the state's support of religion as long as it was disbursed in what they considered to be a fair and equitable way.

In 1702 a new governor, Edward Hyde, Lord Cornbury, arrived in the colony. Described as "vain, irascible and corrupt," Cornbury was thrown into a debtor's prison at the end of his tenure in New York. His personal behavior was an affront to the morality of the age. "It was not uncommon for him to dress himself in a woman's habit and then to patrol the fort in which he resided." Also distinctive was Cornbury's solicitude for the Church of England, which he valued, like Francis Nicholson, for political reasons. "In his zeal for the church he was surpassed by none," wrote an eighteenth-century historian, and, like Nicholson, he was saluted, evidently without sarcasm, as a "Nursing Father of the Church."

Cornbury picked fights with many of the dissenting groups in the colony. He claimed the power to control appointments to the Dutch Reformed Church and forcibly ejected Presbyterians from their church and parsonage in Jamaica, Queens. In 1707 he met his match when he arrested a Presbyterian missionary, Francis Makemie, for preaching in New York without a license. Makemie claimed that he had "liberty" from the Toleration Act of 1689 which did not require him to obtain a license from a colonial governor. Cornbury denied that the Toleration Act applied to the colonies. "I know it is local and limited," he retorted, "for I was at the making thereof." Cornbury imprisoned Makemie for his defiance. Liberated by a writ of habeas corpus, Makemie prevailed against the governor in a trial, despite the jury being instructed by the colony's chief justice, a Cornbury ally, to return a guilty verdict. The despotic Cornbury was relieved of his duties a year later.

Cornbury's highhandedness "strengthened beyond recall the hostility of dissenters to the Anglican settlement." The church grew modestly in subsequent years, supported by a steady stream of S.P.G. missionaries but, numerically, it was overwhelmed by dissenters, who by the middle of the eighteenth century are estimated to have outnumbered it by at least fifteen to one. New York after the Glorious Revolution resembled Maryland and the Carolinas: a weak, established Church of England, which, as the recipient of special favors, was resented by the population at large, coupled with strong and growing dissenting denominations, who, despite government intervention in religious affairs, were satisfied with the level of religious liberty in the colony. Wrote a Dutch parson in 1741: "there is here perfect freedom of conscience for all ... everybody may do what is right in his own eyes, so long as he does not disturb the public peace."

To the east of New York were Connecticut and Massachusetts, colonies settled before the English civil wars by founders motivated by the medieval ideal of compulsive uniformity. Well into the 1680s, these Puritan colonies succeeded in repelling different religions, in suppressing what a Massachusetts minister called "polypiety." In 1680 the governor of Connecticut reported to English authorities that he knew of only ten dissenters in the colony – "four or five seven-day men, ... and about so many more Quakers." Despite fines and imprisonments, Massachusetts authorities had not been able to extinguish a Baptist congregation that moved in 1679 from Noodles Island in Boston harbor to the city itself. But this intrepid congregation seems to have been the only organized group of dissenters in the Bay Colony until Andros imposed an Anglican Church on Boston in 1686.

Massachusetts received a royal government and a new charter in 1691. The charter ordained that "forever hereafter there shall be a liberty of Conscience allowed in the Worshipp of God to all Christians (except Papists) Inhabiting or which shall inhabit or be resident within our said Province or territory." The charter was drawn, according to a distinguished authority "in harmony ... with the spirit of the Toleration Act" and was so interpreted in Massachusetts, with this striking difference: The Congregational Church was considered the established church of the colony, and the established church of the Empire, the Church of England, was viewed as a dissenting domination as were all other churches comprehended under the Toleration Act. Increase Mather, who negotiated the terms of the charter in England, informed the Massachusetts legislators in

1693 that the charter "secured a righteous and generous liberty of conscience . . . and the General Assembly may, by their acts, give a distinguishing encouragement unto that religion which is the general profession of the inhabitants." Mather meant that, aside from the new requirement of liberty of conscience, the assembly could reestablish the Congregational Church on the same basis on which it had existed before the Glorious Revolution and that, specifically, it could require all inhabitants to pay taxes to support it. Thus, in Massachusetts, as elsewhere in the colonies, in the wake of the Toleration Act, liberty of conscience was considered to be compatible with coercive state action in the religious realm. As Congregationalists in the town of Rehoboth, petitioning the assembly in 1726 against Baptists' demands for exemption from religious taxes, stated: The King "has granted Liberty of Conscience to those that worship the True God & yet obligeth the Dissenters of England with their Estates to pay their acknoledgments to the Church their established."

Between 1692 and 1695 Massachusetts legislators, fulfilling their role as "nursing fathers of the church," as the colonies ministers persistently urged them to do, passed laws, reestablishing the Congregational Church, which, disadvantageous as they were to the Church of England, were approved by the King and Council in England. In 1693 New Hampshire passed an act permitting the establishment of the Congregational Church. The statute also acknowledged William and Mary's "grace & favour in Allowing their Subjects liberty of Conscience" and, thirty years in advance of similar developments in Massachusetts and Connecticut, exempted from religious taxes dissenters who "constantly attend the publick worship of God on the Lords day according to their owne Perswassion."

Between 1691 and 1717, Connecticut, whose charter had survived, unscathed, Andros's highhandedness, passed a series of laws, similar to those in Massachusetts, bolstering its Congregational establishment. In 1704 the first dissenting church in Connecticut history was formed at New London – a Baptist congregation, planted by migrants from nearby Rhode Island. The Baptists petitioned the New London County Court for protection under the Toleration Act, and after some hesitation, the Court professed itself willing to accommodate them, if they conformed to the terms of the Act. Historians have speculated that the events in New London may have prompted the Connecticut Assembly in 1708 to pass its own Toleration Act, which stated that those who "soberly dissent" from the Congregational Way and who "qualifie themselves according to an act made in the first year of the late King William and Queen Mary . . . shall enjoy the same libertie and privilege in any place in this colonie without let, or hindrance, or molestation whatsoever," provided they paid taxes to support the established Congregational ministers.

After the Glorious Revolution toleration was the law of the land throughout New England. No less an authority than Cotton Mather pronounced the old regime of compulsive uniformity dead. "New England," declared Mather, "has renounced whatever Laws are against a Just Liberty of Conscience." Perry Miller believed that Mather and his ministerial colleagues protested too much. Their libertarian professions, he wrote, merely proved that "New England was theoretically tolerant." After 1689 the minsters continued to urge the magistrates in the old familiar style to "use all proper means for the suppression of Heresy, Prophaneness and Superstition" and to advance the "truths and ways of God," even though they now lacked the power to compel assent. By the 1730s others in Massachusetts, including Governor Belcher, sent the magistrates a different message, more attuned to current British thinking; they should support religion as a "useful ally of the state because it preserved order and morality."

New England's dissenters were offended by the region's toleration acts. They objected to paying taxes to the dominant church, an issue even more provocative in New England than in the colonies to the south where the Church of England was established. New England Baptists and Quakers considered the Congregational Church as nothing more than a fellow dissenting institution for whose benefit it was particularly galling to be taxed. Some High Church Anglicans took a harsher view. To them, the Congregational Church was "not only invalid, but Sacrilege, and Rebellion against Christ." Why should it receive tax revenues? During the first decades of the eighteenth century, resentment of taxation aroused the dissenters to "unremitting opposition" to the practice, as a result of which the governments of Massachusetts and Connecticut eventually accommodated them.

Who were these dissenters, who represented only a thimbleful of the population before 1689? From whence had they materialized in numbers sufficient to sway legislatures? Massachusetts inherited most of her dissenters from Plymouth, which she absorbed under the new royal government of 1691. That Plymouth had been unable or unwilling to enforce religious uniformity within her borders allowed Quakers to put down roots in some parts of the colony. The most spiritually abandoned part of Plymouth, from Massachusetts' point of view, was Bristol County, which extended to the shores of Narragansett Bay and was culturally and historically aligned with Rhode Island. It contained not only entrenched Quaker meetings, but, almost as bad in Puritan eyes, Baptist churches. After 1691 the Bay Colony was unable to bring these wayward Plymouth settlements to heel, even though the state legislature took direct control of some towns and tried to impose "orthodox" ministers on them. Anglicans arrived in Massachusetts with the new royal government. After 1701 they were served by S.P G. missionaries. All of these dissenting groups actively and continuously lobbied the Massachusetts legislature for tax relief and, when their efforts failed, appealed to well-connected supporters in England who interceded on their behalf with royal officials in London.

Connecticut was beholden to neighboring Rhode Island for most of its dissenters: Baptists, Quakers, and a confrontational sect, known as Rogerenes, whose theology borrowed from both groups and whose radicalism made both appear moderate. Anglicans infiltrated the colony from New York. They achieved a major coup in 1722 by converting the rector of Yale College, Timothy Cutler, and a handful of associates to their confession. As in Massachusetts, local dissenters prodded Connecticut authorities to loosen the ecclesiastical reigns and, failing to achieve results, appealed to supporters in London for assistance.

Beginning in 1727 this pressure, threatening, as it did, reprisals from a royal government always solicitous of the concerns of colonial dissenters, persuaded both Massachusetts and Connecticut to accommodate them on the issue of ecclesiastical taxation. The Puritan colonies moved more or less in tandem, although Connecticut was slightly more generous than Massachusetts. Since Anglicans did not in principle object to taxes for religious purposes, Massachusetts in 1727, followed quickly by Connecticut, directed local tax collectors to turn over to Anglican ministers the church taxes collected from their parishioners living within five miles [two in Connecticut] of their church, a geographical limitation soon dropped. No longer would Anglicans be forced to fund the Congregational Church.

Relief for Quakers and Baptists took a different form. Since these denominations implacably opposed all taxes, they were granted exemptions, provided that their members produced evidence that they were bona fide church members. At the suggestion of the Quakers, certificates issued by denominational officials were accepted by authorities as adequate evidence of membership, although some Baptists chaffed at this procedure. These exemptions made the Baptists and Quakers "far freer than their brethren in England," who paid church taxes well into the nineteenth century, and freer than dissenters in the southern colonies.

An authority on dissenters in New England estimates that by 1735 there were twelve Baptist churches in Massachusetts and Connecticut. Quakers appear "to have been slightly more numerous." There may have been as many as seventeen Anglican churches. Compared to the total population of New England, these numbers were small, but, compared to the pre-1689 number of dissenters, they were huge. To show how far New England had come, consider Boston. In 1747, some eighty years after hanging Quakers, the city had three "pretty large" Anglican churches, "10 large Independent congregations and 3 small congregations, one french upon the Genevan model, one of Anabaptists, and another of Quakers." There were two congregations of the "late humour of separation." An Anglican minister thought that "many" Catholics resided, undetected, in the city.

A survey of the American religious landscape in the mid-1730s, on the eve of the Great Awakening, reveals that the differences in the structure of religion in the various colonies had narrowed since the last of the proprietary governments were added to the American ecclesiastical mix during the reign of Charles II. With the exception of Pennsylvania, New Jersey, and Rhode Island (and Delaware, split from Pennsylvania in 1703), the colonies looked more like each other and, collectively, more like England. In each of them there was an established church, increasingly justified by the English argument of social utility, and in each of them there were legally tolerated dissenters, enjoying religious liberty as it was defined at the time. Unlike England, dissenters were in the majority in some colonies. In all of the colonies, they were present in sufficient numbers and varieties to produce a vigorous pluralism. The majority of dissenters acquiesced in the church settlements in their colonies, although there was everywhere resentment over their inequality of status. On the positive side, members of the church establishment now conceded the dissenters' legitimacy in the social and political order, creating an environment that allowed multiple sects to live together in peace while pursuing their separate religious agendas. Scholars have recently become fond of describing the religious atmosphere in America after 1776 as a "free market" in religion. A free market in religion existed, in fact, in most American colonies, as it did in England, after the passage of the Toleration Act of 1689.

One colony is missing from this picture, a colony whose size and importance make it the elephant in the room: Virginia. Founded like Massachusetts and Connecticut on the ancient principle of coercive uniformity, Virginia attained and perpetuated this ideal much longer than the Puritan colonies. In 1736 a Virginia author bragged that "this government has hitherto enjoied the singular Happiness, that all the Subjects here agree in Uniformity of Worship, according to the doctrine of the Church of England, which is here by Law established; and we have among us no Conventicles or meetings." In 1745 Governor Gooch observed that Virginia was "remarkable for uniformity in worship." It is true that early in the eighteenth century, a few Baptist churches, "like mushrooms in unexpected and out of the way places" sprang up in southeastern Virginia, but they soon disappeared. Few

Virginians were aware of these ephemeral outposts. The uniformity of religion in Virginia in the 1730s exceeded anything achieved in England from Henry VIII's time forward. To find an analogy in the Protestant world, one must turn back to the sixteenth century, to Calvin's Geneva or to Zwingli's Zurich. In eighteenth-century North America, Virginia was a throwback, an ecclesiastical dinosaur.

Virginians were proud that their government promoted the "purest and most edifying Worship of the Church of England." As late as 1772, a member of the Virginia House of Burgesses congratulated his fellow citizens that in the Old Dominion "Christianity has been preserved and inculcated in its greatest Purity, from our earliest Settlements." Did the Virginians' incessant boasting about their "true" and "pure" religion mean that they subscribed to the ancient doctrine of exclusive salvation (i.e., that souls could only be saved within the bosom of the Church of England)? Some may have, but it is far from certain that this conclusion was encouraged by their ministers, who preached morality rather than saving grace. At the very least, Virginians believed that their religion was the "best" available and were not prepared to let outsiders corrupt it. Virginians enthusiastically supported another ancient belief, that enforced uniformity was necessary for social stability. "Many will scarcely believe," said a critic, "that Society can subsist on any Foundation but a Sameness of religion."

The scholar Thomas Buckley has described the religious situation in Virginia in the decade after 1776 as "unique." Compared to its sister colonies, Virginia was unique forty years earlier, a proud Anglican monolith grounded in ideas and practices that had become obsolete in the rest of pluralistic British North America. It should be no surprise that Virginia's reaction to dissenters, whom the Great Awakening first propelled into the colony in the 1740s and who arrived in full evangelical force in the 1760s, was also unique and that the reaction of some of her citizens, foremost of whom were Jefferson and Madison, to this reaction was equally unique.

The Great Awakening (ca. 1739–42) was the first large-scale religious revival in American history, boisterously setting the pattern for all subsequent nationwide revivals. The evangelists who promoted the Awakening considered themselves to be rescuing their fellow Americans from religion gone wrong everywhere in the colonies, religion they accused of gentrifying Christianity by reducing it to personal morality and philanthropy. Fatally missing, in the evangelists' view, was a recognition of the necessity of divine grace, working mysteriously and often disruptively through the holy spirit, to produce the "new birth." The new birth was defined as "A Conviction of Sin and Misery, by the Holy Spirits opening and applying the Law to the Conscience, in order to a saving Closure with Christ." Evangelists traveled throughout the colonies, attempting to awaken their neighbors from their sins and to save them from perdition by transforming them, often through tumultuous emotional encounters with the divine, into the blessed company of the born again. The promoters of the revivals considered the "Screamings, Screeches, Swoonings, Convulsions, Trances, Distractions, Visions and Revelations," which they induced to be unavoidable manifestations of the power of the Holy Spirit.

The Awakeners did not regard themselves as innovators. Jonathan Edwards claimed that he preached nothing but "the common plain Protestant doctrine of the Reformation," a claim accepted by the Awakeners' audiences, who credited them with trying "to restore the Church to the Purity that she professt at the dawn of the Reformation." Revivals were not new. Small ones, including Edwards' Northampton revival, erupted in the Connecticut Valley and in New

Jersey during the first three decades of the eighteenth century. Major revivals had occurred in the British Isles as early as 1625. A Scottish revival in 1742 was described as more frenzied that anything America had seen; "for about an hour and a half there was such weeping and so many falling into deep distress ... that description is impossible. The people seemed to be smitten by the scores. They were carried off and brought into the house like wounded soldiers taken from a field of battle."

What was new about the Great Awakening and what made it great was not the carnival of emotionalism which it inspired but the methods used to promote it and the huge number of Americans who participated in it, either in its first run or in the smaller reruns that continued until the eve of the American Revolution. The impresario of the Great Awakening was George Whitefield, a 25-year-old British evangelical prodigy who electrified the population of several colonies during a prolonged American tour beginning in 1739. Whitefield was greeted in America with the gusto reserved for a modern rock star. A theater buff, he brought the excitement of the British stage to the colonies. John Adams, who heard him as a teenager, called him the "great model of theatrical grace" and claimed that his talents were superior to those of Mrs. Siddons, a legendary figure in the history of the British stage. Americans savored Whitefield because he had the mystique of a rebel. Though an ordained Anglican priest, he abused his superiors – he assailed Archbishop Tillotson for knowing "no more of true religion than Mahomet – and he was contemptuous of Anglican protocols and of attempts to restrict his preaching to authorized places.

Whitefield grasped the importance of advertising that was revolutionizing the world of commerce in his native Britain and employed this powerful tool to revolutionize the presentation of the Word. He promoted his appearances by planting stories in local newspapers, often written by himself, which stressed his previous triumphs, and he used what today would be called public relations techniques to flood preaching venues with his published sermons and religious travelogues. Thus, Whitefield's audiences were primed for the transforming experience of the "new birth," which he preached uncompromisingly, and which often occurred in a self-fulfilling way.

Whitefield attracted incredible crowds as he preached his way through the colonies in 1739–40 (he would return for several more preaching tours). Some 30,000 people were estimated to have heard his farewell sermon in Boston on October 12, 1740, and he enjoyed comparable successes in the middle colonies. Only the south seemed immune to his magic. He admitted that there he found "no stirring among the dry bones," although evangelical groups spawned by his efforts found the southern fields more fertile in the 1750s and 1760s.

The Great Awakening has fascinated modern historians, who have imposed upon it a variety of interpretations. Scholars in the 1960s and 1970s connected it with the American Revolution, arguing that the awakened, born again population acquired antiauthoritarian sentiments, which ripened into a revolutionary mentality in 1776. These views are now out of fashion, but it is indisputable that the Great Awakening had an impact in the American political arena. The reborn, evangelical citizens generated by Whitefield and his American lieutenants split the Congregational churches of New England into pro-and anti-Awakening camps – New Lights and Old Lights – and widened a preexisting chasm in the Presbyterian churches of the middle colonies into similar adversarial groups - New Side and Old Side. The New Lights, the Separate Baptists who evolved from them, and the New Side functioned as freshly minted dissenting groups who were not easily accommodated by the existing church establishments and began, in due time, to demand changes in church-state relations.

New England's Congregational establishment absorbed the first shocks from the Great Awakening. Whitefield and his lieutenants intemperately denounced the established Puritan preachers as unconverted, "dead Men," and advised the newly reborn to leave their worthless ministrations; the new convert, declared Whitefield's "ape," Gilbert Tennent, may "lawfully go and that frequently, where he gets the most good for his precious Soul." It is estimated that as many as ten thousand New Englanders took Tennent's advice and left their local parish churches, forming themselves into one hundred New Light Separatist congregations by the mid-1750s.

The question soon arose: Were the Separatists, or Strict Congregationalists as they often called themselves, a new, bona fide dissenting group, eligible to receive the benefits of the generous system of toleration recently established in New England? Were they, specifically, eligible for the tax relief recently granted to the Anglicans, Quakers, and Baptists? The problem was most acute in Connecticut. Separatists there did not, initially, object to taxation for the support of religion and asked that, like the Anglicans, they be permitted to have their taxes refunded to their own ministers. One of their New Light sympathizers argued in 1742 that "the civil authority are obliged to take care for the support of religion, or in other words, of schools and the gospel ministry, in order to approve themselves nursing fathers," which, he added, "every body will own, and therefore I shall not spend any time proving it." The Separatists contended that it would be tyrannical to force them to pay taxes to the churches "of dead Formality and spiritual Idolatry" which they had just abandoned. Their claims were received with sympathy in a some of the county courts, which administered the Toleration Act of 1708. Angered by the coddling of the New Lights, the Connecticut General Assembly in 1743 stripped the local courts of jurisdiction and assumed control over toleration in the colony, asserting that any group that exhibited a "distinguishing Character" from the established churches would be covered by the Toleration Act of 1689.

In the opinion of Connecticut's legislators, the New Light Separatists were distinguished only by their arrogance and impudence; far from being a new denomination, they were considered to be mere schismatics, beyond the pale of legal toleration. The Separatists did not acquiesce in the assembly's policies. Many refused to pay religious taxes and suffered for it. Their property was seized and sold at public auction to satisfy the tax collector, and many went to jail rather than pay. Others returned to the established churches, many of which had became more hospitable to the New Lights. Connecticut and Massachusetts eventually wore the remaining Separatists down to a small fraction of their numbers at peak strength. The primary reason for their shrinkage, however, was that large numbers of Separatists – half of them, according to some estimates – became Baptists in whose company they had more impact on church–state relations than did the dispirited Separatist remnant.

The Great Awakening was an unexpected blessing for New England's Baptists, who initially opposed it. Most New England Baptists were comparable to the General Baptists in England, conservatives who deplored the emotionalism and strict Calvinism of the Awakeners. These Old Baptists, as they were called in New England, were more sympathetic to the views of "enlightened" Congregationalists like Charles Chauncy than they were to George Whitefield's theatrical flourishes. They were caught off guard when New Light

Separatists began to adopt Baptist principles (believer's baptism, immersion, etc.) and to declare themselves brethren in the faith. The question arose again: Were these New Baptists legitimate dissenters, entitled to the tax exemptions the Old Baptists had won, or were they scoundrels and opportunists who became Baptists to "wash away their taxes."

This problem inflamed communities in Massachusetts and Connecticut but has attracted more attention in the Bay Colony because major political figures such as John Adams were involved in litigating the issue there. The dispute could not be swept under the rug because Separate Baptists in Massachusetts grew rapidly from ten churches in 1740 to sixty-six in 1780 and because they were determined to stand up for their interests. Massachusetts passed a series of acts between 1753 and 1770 that addressed the Separate Baptist claim for tax exemption. Each successive act, though slightly more generous to the Baptists, was inadequate from their perspective. The acts continued the certificate system, requiring Baptists to qualify themselves for tax exemptions by presenting certificates to town officials, signed by a minister and two (originally three) members of the Baptist congregation, attesting that they were members in good standing of the local church. Some towns readily granted the Separate Baptists tax exemptions. In others there were honest disagreements over the interpretation of the controlling statute: Were men and women who regularly attended Baptist churches, but who had not submitted to the signature ritual of immersion, "real" members, entitled to tax exemptions? Elsewhere local officials rejected certificates for nitpicking technicalities (certain words omitted, signatures not in order, etc.). Disputes were particularly acrimonious along Massachusetts's frontiers, where land speculators, who shared the general contempt for the Separate Baptists sect – "a sink for some of the filth of Christianity" – tried to keep them away, lest they lower property values. The Baptists responded in 1773 with what has been described as a campaign of civil disobedience, their leaders urging all members, including those who had received tax exemptions, to refuse to pay taxes and to invite mass imprisonment in hope of embarrassing the authorities into granting sweeping relief.

Leading Congregational clergymen and the political elites in Massachusetts and Connecticut regarded the Separate Baptists as whiners, who complained about a certificate system justly designed to accommodate bona fide dissenters but structured to prevent religious imposters from dodging their taxes. In 1774 Ezra Stiles, the future president of Yale, recorded his exasperation with the Baptists for attacking the Congregationalists of New England, while ignoring the plight of their brethren in Virginia, who, far from receiving tax exemptions, were imprisoned merely for trying to practice their religion in public. "That is," said Stiles, "they forbear to complain where they suffer real Persecution, & complain where they suffer so trifling a share of anything that looks like it."

Stiles was correct that the Baptists suffered "real Persecution" in Virginia, as they tried to spread the message of the Great Awakening there. They were preceded, however, in their evangelical mission to the Old Dominion by New Side Presbyterians, who took the first punches from the colony's monolithic Anglican establishment. Presbyterian activity in Virginia was inspired, indirectly, by Whitefield, who preached in Williamsburg in 1740. In 1743 a "young gentleman from Scotland" shared an edition of the evangelist's sermons, delivered earlier in Glasgow, with citizens of Hanover County, who were awakened to the necessity of the "new birth" and began building "reading houses" to bring the good news to their neighbors. Calling themselves Lutherans, the newly awakened came to the attention of Governor Gooch, bred a Presbyterian in Scotland, who interviewed them and informed them that they were actually Presbyterians and, as such, "were not only tolerated but acknowledged as part of the established church of the realm." When the newly christened Presbyterians sought ministers from New Side authorities in the middle colonies, trouble began.

John Roan was dispatched by the New Siders to Hanover County. According to a nineteenth-century historian, Roan's "spirit took fire and his invectives were not measured." Roan denounced the Anglican Church as "the house of the devil" and assured his audiences that Anglican ministers preached "false doctrine, and that they and all who follow them, are going to hell." Upon receiving word that Roan was "turning the world upside down," Governor Gooch, by all accounts "a mild and tolerant man," determined to stop him, by ordering a grand jury to present Roan on charges ranging from blasphemy to insulting the Anglican liturgy and to seducing the faithful from their allegiance to the established church. Roan prudently fled the colony. Gooch, it should be noted, subscribed to the narrow definition of liberty of conscience prevailing in the eighteenth-century British Empire, by arguing in his grand jury presentment, that toleration of dissenters rested on an implied "covenant" that they would not indulge in "maliciousness" of speech against the Church of England. In Gooch's view, liberty of conscience was compatible, not only with taxation of dissenters but also with limitations on their free speech.

In 1747 another New Side Presbyterian, Samuel Davies, arrived in Virginia, determined to claim the protection of the Toleration Act of 1689 for the evangelical cause. Davies took his case to Gooch and his advisers and discovered that many in Williamsburg contended, like the raffish Lord Cornbury in New York, that the Toleration Act did not apply in the colonies or, at least, not in Virginia. Virginia, they argued, had never adopted the full Toleration Act; at most, it had incorporated only a section in a 1699 statute, relating to church attendance. Others said that the Toleration Act did not cover sects like the New Side, who were not in existence when the act was passed. The Attorney General, Peyton Randolph, initially denied that the Toleration Act was valid in Virginia, an opinion that had strong support in the colony until independence was declared. A writer asserted, for example, in 1771 that he was "one among the few Lawyers in the Country who think you [the dissenters] are entitled to all the Benefit of that Act." Randolph eventually modified his opinion but only to the extent of conceding that the Toleration Act permitted dissenters to minister to a single church, a view fatal to the plans of the itinerant evangelists of the Great Awakening.

Governor Gooch, evidently mindful of his instructions to promote liberty of conscience in the colony, used his influence to obtain for Davies licenses to preach in the reading houses in and around Hanover County. But soon after issuing the licenses, the Gooch administration repented its action. Gooch later told Davies that not only was he unable to obtain a licence for his assistant, John Rodgers, but that "it was with the greatest difficulty he had prevented the recall" of Davies's own licenses. Even when county courts (New Kent, for example) issued licenses to New Side preachers, those licenses were revoked by authorities in Williamsburg. Davies concluded that Virginia intended to strangle the infant New Side movement in its cradle by refusing it the protection of the Toleration

Act, enjoyed by all other dissenters in British North America. He traveled to England in 1753 on what proved to be a futile effort to obtain assistance for the New Side. Back in Virginia, Davies helped the Presbyterian cause by preaching a round of fiery sermons, which roused the spirit of the frontier during the early years of the French and Indian War. These patriotic effusions boosted the reputation of the New Side and gained them a measure of relief from official harassment.

Despite the New Side's anger and frustration at what Davies grandiloquently called the "perpetual susurrations of the ill disposed," its preachers never suffered the "real persecution" which was meted out to the Separate Baptists. It was they who were the unfortunate victims of the "unique" reaction of the monolithic Anglican establishment to their effort to save souls in the Old Dominion.

Separate Baptists arrived in Virginia in 1754, when Shubal Stearns, determined to "carry light into dark places," left his pastorate in Tolland, Connecticut, and traveled with a band of followers to Hampshire County in the mountains of western Virginia. Stearns soon moved to North Carolina, where he enjoyed immediate and spectacular success in planting Separate Baptists congregations in and beyond Guilford County. From their Carolina beachhead, the Separates moved northward, where their converts were as numerous "as the drops of the morning dew." They organized their first congregation in southern Virginia in 1760. By 1767 they had crossed the James River; by 1774 they had increased to 54 congregations.

There were stark differences between the Separate Baptists and New Side Presbyterians. The latter were well educated – Samuel Davies, for example, became president of the College of New Jersey at Princeton upon leaving Virginia – and were the intellectual equals, if not superiors, of their Anglican adversaries. Many Baptist ministers and exhorters were illiterate and proud of it. Baptist services were more unrestrained. A friendly observer said that their "outcries, epilepsies and extacies" – not to mention their visions and prophecies – were "hardly credible." Baptists were more aggressive, often offensively so. Virginians complained that they could "not meet a man upon the road, but they must ram a text of scripture down his throat." They were more abusive, accusing Anglican ministers of being no better than "Pagans and Idolators, who sacrificed their children to Moloch." Finally, they practiced what has been described as a countercultural lifestyle, a "melancholy," austere way of behaving which many Virginians found "menacing, unintelligble."

Because their homogeneous religious culture gave them no reference points to interpret a new mass phenomenon like the Separate Baptists, Virginians employed historical analogies to make sense of them, connecting them to one of the most lurid episodes in Reformation history, the Anabaptist excesses at Munster, Germany, in 1534, which had left an indelible stain on early Protestantism. Seizing Munster, the Anabaptists proclaimed a millennial New Jerusalem, burned books, established a community of goods and wives, elected a "king of the World," and perished in a bloodbath. Ever after, Munster was a symbol of religious hysteria and social anarchy. Anglican authorities talked "about the tenets and practices of the German Anabaptists and assert it as a fact that the present Baptists spring from them." Others compared the Baptists to "Cromwell's roundheads" and claimed that, like the followers of the Lord Protector during the English Civil Wars, their goal was to establish by force a republic in Virginia. Still others brooded that the Baptists meant to "foment a rebellion" or were intent on "carrying on a mutiny against the authority of the land." In 1808 a Baptist described the conclusions produced by the conspiratorial fantasies (common at the time) of their Virginia opponents

> the vain supposition was that when they [the Baptists] once supposed themselves sufficiently strong, that they would fall on their fellow subjects, massacre the inhabitants and take possession of the country . . . it was spoken of from one to another until many of the old bigots would feel their tempers inflamed and their blood run quick in their veins and declare they would take up arms and destroy the New Lights.

Many in the Anglican establishment, clergy and civil authorities acting in concert, backed by mobs, did, in fact take up arms against the Baptists, regarding them as a subversive and destructive force that had, like locusts, suddenly and mysteriously emerged from the soil. This large-scale, state-sponsored violence against the Baptists stigmatized Virginia's reaction to the religious dissent produced by the Great Awakening as unique, for nowhere else in eighteenth-century British North America did anything like this broad, official and forcible wave of repression occur.

Violence began, according to Baptist writers, in 1768 and continued until after independence was declared. A few counties refrained from molesting the Baptists on the theory that they were "like a bed of camomile; the more they were trod, the more they would spread." In many places, however, attempts were made to crush them. The following scene was repeated across the colony: "while at devotion, a mob collected, they immediately rushed upon them in the meeting house, and began to inflict blows, on the worshipers, and produce bruises and bloodshed, so that the floor shone with the sprinkled blood the days following." Often the mobs were led by the sheriff and the local Anglican parson in a display of the power of the church and state united. A diarist recorded how these allies disrupted a Baptist service in Caroline County in 1771:

> While he [the preacher] was Singing the Parson of the parish [who had ridden up with the sheriff] would keep running the End of his Horsewhip in [the preacher's] Mouth. Laying his Whip across the Hym Book, &c. When done singing [the preacher] proceeded to Prayer. In it he was Violently jerked off the Stage. [They] caught him by the Back part of the Neck, Beat his head against the ground, some Times Up, Sometimes down, they Carried him through a Gate that stood some Considerable Distance where a Gentleman [the sheriff] gave him . . . Twenty Lashes with a Horse Whip.

The battered Baptist preachers were then arrested, charged with disturbing the peace, and required to post large bonds, guaranteeing that they would no longer preach in the area. Those who refused to capitulate were thrown into cramped, filthy jails. Efforts were made to poison some and to suffocate others with fumes of a burning concoction of red pepper and tobacco leaves; a plan to blow up a jail holding Baptists miscarried; one Baptist minister reported that his captors urinated in his face.

Like Samuel Davies and the New Siders, the Baptists invoked the Toleration Act to protect themselves. A contemporary Baptist spokesman, Morgan Edwards, refuted a charge that his brethren were responsible for their own persecution because they refused to seek the assistance of the state. According to Edwards, Baptists did, in fact, try to obtain preaching licenses from the authorities under the terms of the Toleration Act. To acquire licenses, the Baptists discovered that they must run a gauntlet unlike anything the Presbyterians confronted.

The English Toleration Act, by delegating the administration of the act to local courts, sought to make the empowerment of dissenters as convenient and trouble-free as possible. In Virginia, however, Baptists (and Presbyterians) were compelled to travel to a "Place far remote," Williamsburg, to qualify before a court that met only twice a year. Additional burdens were laid exclusively on the Baptists. They were required to present a petition signed by twenty freemen and two justices of the peace, attesting to their residency, a document "difficult at all times to obtain." Once in Williamsburg, Baptist applicants were required to pass an examination, testing their theological orthodoxy, administered by an Anglican clergymen. It was extremely difficult, the Baptists claimed, to find any Anglican who would conduct such an examination. Frustrated by a system rigged against them, the Baptists did something that seems uncharacteristic of a sect said to be devoted to the principle of separation of church and state: They asked the government of Virginia for help. Specifically, they petitioned the Virginia Assembly in the winter of 1772, to treat them "with the same kind Indulgence ... as Quakers, Presbyterians, and other Protestant Dissenters enjoy, so far as they relate to allowing the petitioners the same Toleration, in Matters of Religion, as is enjoyed by his Majesty's dissenting Protestant Subjects of Great Britain." The Baptists, in short, demanded equal protection of the law, a law that would give them, equally with other dissenters, the opportunity to conduct, unmolested, religious services under the protection of, and with the permission of, the state.

Apparently embarrassed by the violent persecution of the Baptists as well as by the persistent confusion surrounding the status of the Toleration Act in the colony, the House of Burgesses in March 1772 debated a bill "for extending the benefit of the several acts of toleration to his majestie's protestant subjects of this colony." The bill was a major step forward for the Baptists and Presbyterians, for it recognized their legitimacy as dissenting groups entitled to the protection of the Toleration Act. On the other hand, the bill imposed numerous restrictions on the dissenters, especially on itinerant preaching, which were unacceptable to them and against which they petitioned the assembly for relief. According to James Madison, the bill produced a backlash among supporters of the Anglican establishment and generated a flood of "incredible and extravagant" propaganda against the Baptists, which was "greedily swallowed" by those who were "too much devoted to ecclesiastical establishments to hear of the Toleration of Dissentients."

The toleration bill having failed, violence against the Baptists continued until after independence, fomented by those who wanted to keep the colony purely and exclusively Anglican. Attempts to purge the Baptists were reported as late as 1778, when a Baptist preacher on the eastern shore was imprisoned and then forcibly put aboard a ship whose captain was paid to "make him work his passage over the seas, and then leave him in some countries of Europe." The impression that a steady diet of these outrages made on some of the future leaders of Virginia can be measured by Madison's comments in 1774. To a Pennsylvania correspondent he wrote that the

> diabolical Hell conceived principle of persecution rages among some and to their eternal Infamy the Clergy can furnish their Quota of Imps for this business. . . . I have neither patience to hear talk or think of any thing relative to this matter, for I have squabbled and scolded abused and ridiculed so long about it . . . that I am without common patience.

No spirit of prophecy is required to predict Madison's attitude toward church establishments in the new American republic.

Scholars have tended to exaggerate the impact of the Great Awakening on the church–state relations in colonial America. In New

England and Virginia, where the evangelical population produced by the Awakening was the largest and most assertive, the demands of most New Lights, New Siders, and Separate Baptists rarely went beyond agitation for improvements in their status as tolerated minorities in a system of established state churches. In New England this meant a blanket exemption for the Separate Baptists from ecclesiastical taxes. In Virginia the objective was the more modest one of the legitimization of dissent.

Large numbers of Virginians, members of the assembly and dissenters alike, were comfortable with the definition of liberty of conscience that had been popularized by eighteenth-century British dissenters: freedom from forcible interference with public worship coupled with acquiescence in state intervention in other aspects of religion. Consider in this respect a petition to the House of Burgesses, May 17, 1774, from Bedford County Presbyterians in which the petitioners endorsed the compatibility between liberty of conscience and the state's imposition of taxes to support the Church of England. "Your petitioners," wrote the Bedford Presbyterians, "have in times past and are still willing to contribute their Quota in support of the Church of England . . . which they do with more cheerfulness, as they have hitherto enjoyed their Rights and Privileges and free exercise of their Religion as Dissenters unmolested." There is no record of any written objection by Virginia Baptists to state-imposed religious taxes before 1776.

There were unmistakable signs, however, that as the American Revolution approached, dissenters in Virginia, New England, and elsewhere in America were beginning to entertain larger conceptions of religious freedom. On June 5, 1774, members of the Hanover Presbytery, a more authoritative body than their Bedford brethren, submitted a petition to the House of Burgesses dissecting the toleration bill of 1772. The Hanover Presbytery identified a number of shortcomings in the bill that offended against equality. The Presbytery asserted that "as long as our fellow-subjects are permitted to meet together by day and or by night" its members should have the same privilege; penalties for miscreants who disturbed Presbyterian worship services should be "the same as those who disturb the congregation or misuse the preachers of the Church of England"; Presbyterians should, in short, have "as ample priviledges as any of our fellow subjects enjoy." They should, in fact, have nothing less than "equal liberty."

The claim to equal religious status with "fellow subjects," the conviction that the privileged position of the Church of England was contrary to "our first notions of justice and equality," was undoubtedly inspired by the egalitarian political rhetoric percolating throughout the colonies in the run-up to the American Revolution. On the eve of the Revolution, Americans throughout the colonies were demanding equal rights with their fellow citizens in Britain and with each other in the spiritual as well as the secular sphere. The demand for equal rights, grounded in the law of nature, was a challenge to the survival of the colonial establishments, which were, of course, based on favoritism toward one denomination. Could these establishments survive – should they survive – in a world of equal, rights-bearing citizens? Or could they be modified to accommodate the contagious claims for equality? These questions arose as soon as independence was declared in 1776.

One issue did not arise before 1776: the separation of church and state. Scholars have shown that dissenters battling the colonial establishments did not entertain such an idea. William McLoughlin, the authority on New England dissenters, asserted "that the Separate-Baptists, like the Old Baptists and the Separatists before them, did not have a clearly defined conception of separation of church and state when they began their struggle." Philip Hamburger has recently demonstrated that colonial dissenters would have been insulted had they been accused of favoring the separation of church and state. An even stronger verdict was delivered by the Baptist scholar, R. E. Harkness, who scoffed at a speech purportedly made by Patrick Henry in 1768 in which Henry allegedly advocated the separation of church and state. "No man in America ever thought or spoke in such terms in 1768," Harkness declared. Not until after Henry's death in 1799 would "such terms" enter American public discourse.

3

The Confederation Period

THE FIRST CONTINENTAL CONGRESS, WHICH PUT THE American colonies on the path to independence from Great Britain, convened in Philadelphia on September 5, 1774. Fifty-five delegates, representing twelve colonies, attended. On the morning of September 6, Thomas Cushing of Massachusetts moved that proceedings begin with a prayer. Objections were immediately raised that "We were so divided in religious Sentiments, some Episcopalians, some Quakers, some Anabaptists, some Presbyterians and some Congregationalists . . . that we could not join in the same Act of Worship." Declaring that he was "no Bigot," Samuel Adams, an old-fashioned Puritan, made an ecumenical recommendation that a local Anglican priest, Jacob Duche, be asked to officiate in Congress the next morning. Duche, who defected to the British in 1777, led Congress in a moving prayer service on September 7. This episode reveals that by 1774 pluralism had become a distinguishing feature of American religion and that Congress would embrace religion at its earliest opportunity.

The Continental and Confederation Congresses (1774–89) were full of deeply religious men in positions of leadership. Charles Thomson, the soul of Congress and the source of its institutional continuity as its permanent secretary from 1774 to 1789, retired from public life to translate the Scriptures from Greek into English; the four-volume Bible that Thomson published in 1808 is admired by modern scholars for its accuracy and learning. John Dickinson, who, as the "Pennsylvania Farmer," was the colonies' premier political pamphleteer, and who, as a member of Congress in 1776, wrote the first draft of the Articles of Confederation, also retired from public life to devote himself to religious scholarship, writing commentaries on the Gospel of Matthew. So did Elias Boudinot, president of Congress, 1782–3, who tuned out "warm" debates on the floor to write his daughter long letters, praying that, through the blood of God's "too greatly despised Son," she should be "born again to the newness of life." Resigning as Director of the United States Mint in 1805, Boudinot wrote religious tracts such as *The Second Advent* (1815) and the next year became the first president of the American Bible Society.

Henry Laurens, president of Congress, 1777–8, was "strict and exemplary" in his performance of religious duties. He "read the scriptures diligently to his family" and "made all his children read them also. His family Bible contained in his own handwriting several of his remarks on passing providences." John Jay, Laurens's successor as president of Congress, 1778–9, and later first chief justice of the Supreme Court, was extolled for the "firmness, even fervor, of his religious conviction." When he retired from public life, he also became president of the American Bible Society (1821). Even the two congressmen who defected to the British were conspicuous for their religious, if not their patriotic, ardor: John Joachim Zubly of Georgia was a Presbyterian minister and Joseph Galloway of Pennsylvania, a major figure at the First Continental Congress, later published commentaries on the Book of Revelations, which he prescribed as a "pill for the infidel and atheist."

It should not be surprising that these faithful men and their deeply religious colleagues injected strong elements of Christianity into the proceedings of the Continental and Confederation Congresses. They were urged on by Duche, who ministered to Congress in an unofficial capacity until he was elected its first chaplain on July 9, 1776. "Go on, ye chosen band of Christians," Duche entreated the members in 1775. And go on they did, regularly acting as a committee of lay ministers, preaching to the people of the United States as a national congregation, pressing them to act like the Christians they professed to be by confessing their sins, repenting, and bearing fruits befitting repentance.

On June 12, 1775, Congress announced that July 20 would be the first national day of "public humiliation, fasting and prayer." Its conveyed its decision to state authorities and then to the churches, establishing a channel that it repeatedly used to communicate with the nation's citizens. On May 8, for example, Congress issued an assessment of the country's political and military situation which it ordered to be read by "ministers of the gospel of all denominations . . . immediately after divine services." By participating in this process, year in and year out, the clergy became the political auxiliaries of Congress.

The "Continental fast" of July 20 did not disappoint those like John Adams, who predicted that "Millions will be on their Knees at once before the great Creator, imploring his Forgiveness and Blessing, His Smiles on American Councils and Arms." On the appointed day, Congress attended services in a body and heard sermons in the morning at Duche's Anglican Church and in the afternoon at Francis Allison's Presbyterian meeting, being careful, as it was throughout the war, not to patronize exclusively any one denomination, lest it be accused of religious favoritism, a red flag in a nation now committed to the equality of all (Christian) religions. Later Congress worshiped en masse at Philadelphia's "Roman Chapel," July 4, 1779, and at the "Dutch Lutheran Church," October 24, 1781. In an additional effort to appear even-handed in religious matters, Congress, after Duche's defection in 1777, appointed joint chaplains of different denominations.

Certain phrases in Congress's proclamation of June 12, scheduling the July 20 fast – God's "desolating judgements," "confess and deplore our many sins," "beseech him to forgive our iniquities," "implore his merciful interposition for our deliverance" – have tipped scholars off that Congress had adopted and was expounding the venerable religious doctrine called "covenant theology." As old as the Reformation itself, this doctrine was embraced by all of the major Protestant groups who settled America, although some scholars have made it synonymous with New England Congregationalism.

Covenant theology was simplicity itself. It held that God had condescended to bind Himself to human beings by what amounted to a legal agreement – a covenant – to reward their faithfulness or to punish their sins. Preachers explained that, as parties to a covenant, "a people should be prosperous or afflicted, according as their general Obedience or Disobedience thereto appears." God might visit a sinful people with natural afflictions – floods, droughts, epidemics – or political ones – oppression, rebellion, war. Although secular men might ascribe the conflict with the mother country to a conspiracy of rapacious British politicians, religious Americans knew better. As a preacher explained, "in seasons of great difficulty and distress we are apt to look too much to second causes, and to forget that whatever evil or calamity is brought upon us, the hand of the Lord is in it."

For ten years, from its first fast day proclamation of June 12, 1775, until its final thanksgiving proclamation of August 3, 1784, Congress adopted and preached to the American people the political theology of the national covenant, settling into a pattern of issuing a fast day proclamation every March and a thanksgiving proclamation every October. Selections from various fast day proclamations show how Congress, guided by covenant theology, drew the roadmap America must follow to retain God's favor. The first requirement was that the American people recognize God's "overruling Providence" (1776); then they must acknowledge that the war and its attendant evils were God's chastisements for the nation's sins, it having pleased God "for the punishment of our manifold offenses, to permit the sword of war still to harrass our country" (1780); next they must "confess and bewail our manifold sins and trespasses" (1776) and exhibit "sincere repentance and amendment of life [to] appease his righteous displeasure" (1781); finally, they should look for deliverance, hoping "that it may please the Lord of Hosts, the God of Armies, to animate our officers and soldiers with invincible fortitude ... and to crown the continental arms, by sea and land, with victory and success." (1776).

The language of the congressional proclamations was unapologetically Christian. Congress specifically sought the intervention on the nation's behalf of Jesus Christ, praying God in 1776 "through the merits and mediation of Jesus Christ [to] obtain his pardon and forgiveness" and inviting its fellow Americans in 1777 to "join the penitent confession of their manifold sins ... and their humble and earnest supplication that it may please God, through the merits of Jesus Christ, mercifully to forgive and blot them out of remembrance."

As urgent and as eloquent as the congressional proclamations were, compliance with them, as with the requisitions Congress submitted to the states to raise money, was voluntary. Congress depended on the good will of the nation's churches to give effect to its proclamations. It had no power, it had no resources at its disposal, to create a religious citizenry, to assure that "pure, undefiled religion, may universally prevail" in America, an indispensable condition, it asserted in 1776, for enlisting God on the side of the new American nation.

One area in which Congress did have power was the control of the armed forces, and here it did everything that it could to produce a pious military. In the Articles of War, governing the conduct of the Continental Army, adopted on June 30, 1775, and revised and expanded on September 20, 1776, Congress devoted three of the four articles in the first section to the religious nurture of the troops. In Article 2 it was "earnestly recommended to all officers and soldiers to attend divine services." Punishment was prescribed for those who behaved "indecently or irreverently" in churches, including courts-martial, fines, and imprisonments; chaplains who deserted their troops were court-martialed.

Congress feared the navy as a source of moral corruption and demanded that skippers of American ships make their men behave. The first article in Rules for the Regulation of the Navy, adopted on November 28, 1775, ordered all commanders "to shew themselves a good example of honor and virtue to their officers and men and . . . to discountenance and suppress all dissolute, immoral and disorderly practices." The second article required those same commanders "to take care, that divine services be performed twice a day on board, and a sermon preached on Sundays." Article 3 prescribed punishments for swearers and blasphemers: Offending officers were to be fined, and common sailors were to be forced "to wear a wooden collar or some other shameful badge of distinction."

It is difficult to overemphasize Congress's concern for the spiritual condition of the armed forces because the covenant mentality convinced it that irreligion in the ranks was, of all places, the most dangerous, for God might directly punish a backsliding military with defeat, extinguishing in the process American independence. Congress expressed its anxiety in its fast day proclamation of December 11, 1776, recommending "in the most earnest manner" to "officers civil and military under them, the exercise of repentance and reformation; and further, require of them the strict observation of the articles of war, and particularly, that part of the said articles, which forbids profane swearing, and all immorality."

An unfailing antidote to immorality was Bible reading. Hostilities, however, had interrupted the supply of Bibles from Great Britain, raising fears of a shortage of Scripture just when it was needed most. In the summer of 1777 three Presbyterian ministers alerted Congress to the problem and urged it to arrange for a domestic printing of the Bible. Upon investigation, a committee of Congress discovered that it would be cheaper to import Bibles from Europe and made such a recommendation to the full Congress on September 11, 1777. Congress approved the recommendation the same day, instructing its Committee of Commerce to import twenty thousand Bibles from "Scotland, Holland or elsewhere" but adjourned – the British were poised to take Philadelphia – without passing implementing legislation.

The issue of the Bible supply was raised again in Congress in 1780 when it was moved that the states be requested "to procure one or more new and correct editions of the Old and New Testaments to be published." The committee to whom this motion was referred was in due course charged with evaluating a petition (January 21, 1781) from a Philadelphia printer, Robert Aitken, that the national legislature officially sanction a publication of the Old and New Testaments that he was preparing at his own expense. By September 1, 1782, Aitkin's Bible was finished and Congress asked its chaplains, the Episcopalian William White and the Presbyterian George Duffield, to evaluate it. Having received the chaplains' report on September 10 that Aitken had done his work with "great accuracy," Congress on September 12 passed the following resolution: "The United States in Congress assembled, highly approve the pious and laudable undertaking of Mr. Aitken, as subservient to the interest of religion . . . and being satisfied from the above report, of his care and accuracy in the execution of the work, they recommend this edition of the Bible to the inhabitants of the United States." Aitken's edition of the Scriptures, published under congregational patronage, appeared shortly thereafter. It was the first English language Bible published on the North American continent.

A Congress constantly exhorting its constituents to promote the spread of Christianity, to spare no efforts, as its fast day proclamation of March 19, 1782, urged, to ensure that the "religion of our Divine Redeemer . . . covers the earth as the waters cover the seas," could not be indifferent to the cause of Christ in the vast new territories, stretching from the Allegheny Mountains to the Mississippi River, acquired from Britain in the peace settlement of 1783. Accordingly, when Congress, in the spring of 1785, debated regulations for selling property in the new lands, delegates from New England, where the state had always financed the work of the church, moved that the central section in each township should be reserved for the support of schools and "the section immediately adjoining the same to the northward, for the support of religion. The profits arising therefrom in both instances, to be applied for ever according to the will of the majority." According to James Madison this proposal "received the countenance" of a congressional committee but was not enacted into law. A grant of government land to support religion did pass, however, on July 27, 1787, when Congress voted that ten thousand acres on the Muskingum River in the present state of Ohio "be set apart and the property thereof be vested in the Moravian brethren ... or a society of the Brethren for civilizing the Indians and promoting Christianity."

Under what authority did Congress conduct its wide-ranging activities in religion, its sermonizing the country, its sponsoring a Bible, and its appointing chaplains for civilian and military duty, its granting public land to promote Christianity? Nowhere in the Articles of Confederation was there even a hint of a congressional power to regulate religion. Yet the citizens at large made no objections to Congress's efforts to promote religion. Why did they not?

Madison furnished an answer in *Federalist* 38, in discussing Congress's administration of the northwest territories. Everything that Congress did in establishing mechanisms for governing the Old Northwest, Madison observed, was "done without the least color of constitutional authority. Yet no blame has been whispered; no alarm has been sounded." Why not? Because, Madison explained, "the public interest, the necessity of the case, imposed upon them the task of overleaping their constitutional limits." Just so with religion. Congress overleaped the limitations on its activity in the religious sphere and escaped censure because its constituents approved of its efforts to encourage nonsectarian religious practice as promoting the public interest. Religion, Congress asserted in the Northwest Ordinance of 1787, was one of the principal elements "necessary to good government and the happiness of mankind."

Congress's support for religion was principally rhetorical. It did not attempt to exercise coercive powers because it had none. Under the Articles of Confederation the states retained their sovereignty and the full panoply of power attendant thereupon. They could lay religious taxes, punish dissent, require church attendance; they could, in short, do everything in the religious realm that the British government could do. The Declaration of Independence did not magically terminate the religious disputes that the states inherited from their colonial pasts. In their efforts to resolve these disputes, the states, not the weak national government under the Articles, set the future course of government–religion relations in the United States.

Historians, who have tried to show how "revolutionary," how "radical," the American Revolution was, habitually cite the efforts of the new state governments to disestablish religion to support their thesis. J. Franklin Jameson in his influential book, *The American Revolution Considered as a Social Movement* (1926) was one of the first to insist on this point; Bernard Bailyn in his path-breaking *Ideological Origins of the American Revolution* (1967) emphasized it. Readers of volumes of the "radicalizing" Revolution genre could easily conclude that as soon as the ink dried on the Declaration of Independence the states uniformly sprang into action to obliterate their prewar religious establishments. In 1986 the formidable constitutional scholar, Leonard Levy, deflated this thesis by showing that "after the American Revolution seven of the fourteen states that comprised the Union in 1791 authorized establishments of religion by law."

Although Levy used the term "establishment" in a tendentious manner to support a pet thesis about the meaning of the First Amendment, the thrust of his argument – that after the Revolution half of the states tried to find ways to offer meaningful support to religion – is correct. Levy documented his claim in the following manner: Before the Revolution nine of the thirteen American states had religious establishments; after 1776, two of these states, North Carolina and New York, in which dissenters dominated, disestablished the Church of England, joining Pennsylvania, Delaware, New Jersey, and Rhode Island in the ranks of states without established churches. Six of the remaining seven states with prewar establishments either passed laws or inserted clauses in their new constitutions, permitting their governments to offer financial or other kinds of support to their churches. In the seventh state with a prewar establishment, Virginia, a bill to provide financial assistance would have passed, apparently, had Patrick Henry, its chief sponsor and promoter, not left the House of Delegates to become governor. If Vermont, which entered the Union in 1791 with a loosely established church, is added to the original thirteen, seven states (Levy's figure) had succeeded at some point after 1776 in authorizing meaningful assistance to their churches, and an eighth, Virginia, had come very close to doing so. To claim or imply that the Declaration of Independence ignited a headlong, nationwide effort to sever the ligaments between government and religion is simply not true.

There can be no mystery why, after July 4, 1776, large numbers of Americans wanted their new state governments to continue patronizing religion. The Declaration of Independence did not repeal the Old Testament or subvert the wisdom of the ages. Isaiah 49:23, requiring civil rulers to be nursing fathers of the church, spoke to Americans as authoritatively after July 4 as before, and the immemorial conviction that religion was essential to the civil utility of a nation by producing morally sound, law-abiding citizens – the building blocks of the good society – continued to appear self evident to most people.

After independence was declared, politicians, preachers, and newspaper scribblers bombarded the public with the nursing fathers metaphor, especially in states where churches had been established in the colonial period. On September 13, 1783, the *Virginia Gazette, or, The American Advertiser* published an article, claiming to represent the "sentiments of the judicious Christians in this State," who were unhappy that in the Old Dominion "the friendly aid of the Legislature" had not yet been bestowed on religion. "Far be it from us," the judicious Christians declared, "to suppose that you [the legislators] conceive it beneath your dignity, to become nursing fathers of the church, and to promote true piety and devotion amongst us." In the same vein the citizens of Amherst County urged the General Assembly on November 27, 1783, not to "think it beneath your Dignity to become Nursing Fathers of the Church."

In New England Ezra Stiles in his widely read sermon, *The Unites States Elevated to Glory and Honor* (1783), appealed to his audience, the members of the Connecticut General Assembly, not to "repudiate the idea of being nursing fathers to our spiritual Israel, the church of God within this state. Give us, gentlemen," Stiles continued, "the decided assurance that you are friends of the churches, and that you are friends of the pastors." A member of the Massachusetts Constitutional Convention of 1780 disclosed that on the convention floor one of the principal arguments for the continuation of public funding for the state's Congregational ministers was the reminder "that the prophet Isaiah, in speaking of gospel times, had declared, that kings should become nursing fathers and queens nursing mothers to the church; which most certainly implied, that the civil authority would make suitable provision for the support and maintenance of public worship and teachers of religion."

Were these incessant entreaties to policymakers to play the nursing father to the churches effective? Opponents of state-supported religion thought they were. Isaac Backus, the Massachusetts Baptist leader, asserted that one of the reasons for the success of the advocates of state support in New England was their ability to "plead . . . that promise to the church, that Kings shall be thy nursing fathers and that Queens her nursing mothers." In Virginia another Baptist leader, John Leland, testified to the power of the nursing fathers metaphor. Reflecting in 1791 on his recently concluded fourteen-year pastorate in Virginia, Leland observed that the "rulers" there had been swayed by the Isaiah passage to endorse the public funding of religion on the grounds that it would be "advantageous to the state" and that "this they often do the more readily when they are flattered by the clergy that if they thus defend the truth they will become nursing fathers of the church and merit something considerable for themselves."

The nursing fathers metaphor was used against Leland's friend, Thomas Jefferson, who was smeared as an "atheist," when he ran for president in 1800. During the campaign, John Mitchell Mason, a popular Presbyterian minister in New York City and a founder of Union Theological Seminary, admonished his fellow citizens that

> you are commanded to pray for your rulers . . . You entreat him [God] to fulfill his promise, that kings shall be to his church nursing-fathers and queens her nursing mothers. With what conscience can you lift your hands in such a supplication, when you are exerting yourselves to procure a president who does not fear God . . . do you think the church of Christ is to be nurtured by the dragon's milk of infidelity?"

In addition to discharging a scriptural obligation, officials and lawmakers in the new state governments proposed to grant their churches financial or other forms of support because of the widespread belief that religion served the "public utility," a term that many Americans preferred, after 1776, to the British term, "civil utility," although that phase did not disappear from public discourse. By the 1760s Americans had become comfortable with the British practice of emphasizing religion's role as an ally of government. In 1765, for example, a Connecticut Congregational minister, Edward Dorr, preached an election sermon, entitled *The Duty of Civil Rulers, to be nursing Fathers to the Church of Christ*, in which he argued "that the public profession and practice of religion, was a benefit to the state, and absolutely necessary to the safety and security of civil government." This kind of reasoning mushroomed after 1776, finding advocates even in Pennsylvania and New Jersey. It was stressed so vigorously in some quarters that many appeared to be flirting with Warburton's view that the sole purpose of religion was to buttress the state. Ezra Stiles was one of those who feared, after 1776, that the emphasis on the public utility of religion had become excessive, lamenting in 1783 the scarcity of the "Christian patriot, who from his heart wishes the advancement of Christianity much less for the civil good than for the eternal welfare of immortal souls."

Recognition of the public utility of religion, Americans after independence emphasized, dated far back into antiquity. "The most approved and wisest legislators in all ages," wrote a Virginian in 1784, "in order to give efficacy to their civil institutions, have found it necessary to call in the aid of religion" as "an assistant to civil Government." That religion was "a most valuable security to state," asserted a Pennsylvanian in 1787, "is an opinion held not only by all good and wise in the world ... [but by] truly great minds in every country and age." The next year a South Carolinian claimed that "a transient view of the states and kingdoms, which have made the most striking figure in the history of the world ... will convince us that religion was by them always considered as a matter of great importance

to civil society. The greatest politicians and most celebrated legislators of antiquity much depended on this to give sanction to their
laws, and make them operate with vigour and facility."

The most celebrated legislator in the United States, George Washington, forcefully endorsed the public utility of religion. "True religion," Washington informed a synod of the Dutch Reformed Church
in October 1789, "affords government its surest support." With the
whole nation as his audience, Washington repeated these sentiments
in his Farewell Address, September 19, 1796. "Religion and morality," said the retiring hero, "are indispensable supports [of] political
prosperity" and "great Pillars of human happiness."

The Congress of the Confederation repeatedly delivered the same
message: "true religion and good morals are the only solid foundation
of public liberty and happiness" (1778); a "universal reformation"
in religion would "make us a holy, that we may be a happy people" (1782); and "the practice of pure and undefiled religion ... is
the great foundation of public prosperity and national happiness"
(1782). The much admired Massachusetts Constitution of 1780 contributed to the drumbeat by declaring that "the happiness of a people,
and the good order and preservation of civil government, essentially
depend on piety, religion, and morality," language borrowed by the
Maryland House of Delegates in an Address, January 8, 1785, to
the citizens of the state, in which the House asked "where shall
we find a system of religion which conduces so effectually to good
order, peace [and] happiness of society, as the religion of Christ?"
The New Hampshire Constitution of 1784 incorporated the Massachusetts language, adding that "evangelical principles will give
the best and greatest security to government."

These official testimonials were but the tip of the iceberg.
Hundreds of statements were made between 1776 and 1787, by

Americans in every profession and from every state, testifying to the power of religion to bring about a litany of public goods: happiness, prosperity, liberty, good government, peace, and order. There was no problem in identifying the asset that enabled religion to "produce those effects which are confessed to be of such singular service." It was the doctrine of the "future state of rewards and punishment," and it operated, according to Americans who promoted it after 1776, exactly as Warburton had described it in 1737, and as its advocates, stretching back to a time "before we have any light into antiquity," had employed it. It informed the population that, in the afterlife, sublime rewards or unspeakable punishments awaited, for all eternity, those who were good or bad during their time on earth. Who could doubt that it paid – and paid in the currency of everlasting life – to be good?

Several states wrote the future rewards and punishment doctrine into their new republican constitutions, their purposes being to secure virtuous voters, elected officials, and bureaucrats. The Pennsylvania Constitution of 1776 and the Vermont Constitution of 1777 required members of their Houses of Representatives to swear an oath, affirming their belief in a future state. The South Carolina Constitution of 1778 required voters to believe in a future state. The first draft of the Massachusetts Constitution of 1780 affirmed that "the knowledge and belief of the being of God, his providential government of the world, and of a future state of rewards and punishments, [were] the only true foundation of morality." The 1785 Constitution of the abortive state of Franklin in western North Carolina and the 1796 Constitution of Tennessee both required officials in their "civil department" to believe in a future state of rewards and punishments. The future state doctrine had strong support in other states. In 1779 the Virginia House of Delegates came close to passing a bill that would have offered financial subsidies to the state's denominations, if they affirmed "that there is one Eternal God and a future state of rewards and punishments." In 1785 Maryland's House of Delegates declared that "government can have no confidence in that man who is under no religious ties, and who believes in neither Heaven nor Hell, or, in other words, a future state of rewards and punishments."

Most of the proponents of the future state doctrine borrowed their material from British authors like Warburton and Bolingbroke. Some Americans, however, displayed originality by injecting Islam into the discourse. The Reverend Samuel West, for example, a member of the Massachusetts Constitutional Convention, writing in *Boston Gazette*, November 27, 1780, observed that, although "all those doctrines and parts of worship" in the state's Christian churches were "really necessary for the well-being of civil society . . .

> perhaps no one is of greater importance to promote the peace and safety of the community than the doctrine of a future state of reward and punishment; for we shall find that persons are often restrained from gross immoralities by the fear of future miseries, when civil penalties prove insufficient for that purpose. A doctrine of such amazing importance to promote the civil good of society ought to be very strongly impress'd upon the minds of men in order to render it beneficial to society.
>
> We find that a future state of rewards and punishments . . . when it has been taught and impressed upon the minds of any people according to the received standard of their religious belief, has undoubtedly produced beneficial effects to society. Thus a Mahometan is excited to the practice of good morals in hopes that after the resurrection he shall enjoy the beautiful girls of paradise to all eternity. He is afraid to commit murder, adultery, & theft lest he be cast into hell, where he must drink scalding water and the scum of the damned & have nothing to breathe but terrible hot and suffocating air.

Benjamin Rush, a close friend of both Adams and Jefferson, echoed West, when he wrote in 1786 that "such is my veneration for every religion that reveals the attributes of the Deity, or a future state of rewards and punishments, that I had rather see the opinions of Confucius or Mohammed inculcated upon our youth than see them grow up wholly devoid of a system of religious principle."

Despite these tips of the hat to Islam, few Americans believed that the religion of Mohammed or any other religion known to man could compare with Christianity as a motivator of good behavior. As Thomas Reese, a South Carolina Presbyterian minister, wrote in 1788: "Christianity exhibits the most terrible and striking picture of that punishment which will be inflicted on the wicked." Heathen writers, including geniuses like Homer and Virgil, "who had tried their strength and exerted the whole force of their talents, in describing a future state" were no match for the gospel writers. "What are these," Reese continued,

> when compared to the descriptions which the pen of inspiration gives us of hell, the seat of enraged justice and burning vengeance, and of those eternal pains which the enkindled wrath of the almighty inflicts upon the wicked ghosts, who are condemned to those gloomy mansions of endless horror and despair.... What gloomy and dreadful images are these! How awfully grand and striking! How well accommodated to awaken our fears, to deter us from evil, and to stimulate us to the practice of piety and virtue.

Here was the key to all of the profuse praise, in the years after 1776, of the "public utility" of religion: Armed with the doctrine of the future state of rewards and punishments, it was expected, by irresistible appeals to self-interest, to stimulate the practice of piety and virtue, which would produce "good men" who, no one doubted, "must be good citizens." In Reese's words, "if you be good Christians, you can never fail of being good citizens." Bishop James Madison of Virginia asserted that religion produced "the perfection of citizens." There are a multitude of statements after 1776 about Christianity's ability to make Americans "good citizens," "good members of society," "the most industrious and wise citizens." As early as 1756 a young John Adams saluted Christianity for creating "good men, good magestrates and good Subjects." In 1789 George Washington congratulated religious leaders for their power to produce "sober, honest and good citizens and obedient subjects of a lawful government."

If religion did its job, it would create a body politic with a critical mass of good, virtuous people who would provide the human capital that could secure all the public benefits Americans sought to achieve after 1776 – happiness, peace, order, and so on. Religion was also expected to undergird republicanism, the objective for which, after independence, the war with Britain was fought. In an oft-quoted statement, accurately expressing American opinion, Benjamin Rush informed Thomas Jefferson in 1800 that he "always considered Christianity as the *strong ground* of republicanism." What Rush meant was that he and other Americans, rather than regarding republicanism as a particular form of government, conceived of it as an animating principle, that principle being virtue infused throughout the body politic. As the principal source of virtue and good citizenship, religion was considered by Rush and many others to be essential to the success of the republican experiment in the United States.

One last public policy benefit conferred by a virtuous body of citizens emanated from the transcendent level. Insofar as religion, employing the future state doctrine, created a virtuous society, so far did that society uphold with God its end of the covenant bargain, whose fulfillment was of such anxious and continuing concern to the Continental and Confederation Congresses. It was axiomatic that God rewarded the "obedience of His chosen covenanted people with prosperity and their disobedience with adversity." If God could be counted on to reward a society obedient to his will – which no one doubted – then that society must be one in which vibrant, all-encompassing religion prevailed.

If public support for religion was a scriptural obligation, a policy recommended by the greatest political theorists and leaders of all ages, and a panacea for the social and political problems the new American state and national governments were facing – or might be expected to face in the future – should it not have been, after 1776, a "no-brainer" for Americans to embrace the idea? Opponents had a ready answer: They had heard it all before. The arguments for public support of religion had been used, especially from the mid-eighteenth century onward, as the rationale for taxing dissenters to support the colonial establishments. A new age dawned in America on July 4, 1776, when Congress announced to the world that all men were created equal. Dissenters were no longer prepared to suffer the discrimination of being taxed to support another man's religion. Indeed, they were no longer prepared to be stigmatized as dissenters. They made it unmistakably clear that they would accept nothing less than full equality in religious matters which, in their view, required major changes in the policies to which they had been subjected before 1776.

Independence aroused Americans to convene conventions to write new republican constitutions. Dissenters [when used here-after, *prewar* dissenters (i.e., Baptists and Presbyterians) are meant] insisted that their lawmakers satisfy their concerns. "Yield to the mighty current of American freedom," the Presbyterian leader of South Carolina's dissenters, William Tennent, urged the state's assembly in 1777: give us "Equality or Nothing." In Virginia on October 16, 1776, the General Association of Baptists presented a petition, five feet long, signed by ten thousand citizens, demanding "Equal Liberty! That invaluable blessing: which though it be the birthright of every good Member of the State has been what your Petitioners have been deprived of, in that, by Taxation their Property has been wrested from them and given to those from whom they have received no equivalent." In New England dissenters peppered their representatives with pleas for "equal liberty of conscience" and "equal Christian liberty." Describing the years after 1776, a Philadelphia magazine in 1787 claimed that "the idea of equality breathes through the whole and every individual feels ambitious to be in a situation not inferior to his neighbour." A scholar has written that "at the heart" of the quest for independence and republicanism "lay equality, the most powerful and influential concept in American history." After 1776 this concept was as potent in the religious as in the civil precincts of American life.

Virginia offers a good example of how lawmakers accommodated the swelling demands for equality. George Mason's first draft of the Virginia Declaration of Rights, May 20–26, 1776, addressed the religious issue by stipulating that "all men should enjoy the fullest toleration in the exercise of religion, according to the dictates of conscience," language which appears to indicate that Mason, a noted libertarian, accepted the contemporary British view that toleration conferred liberty of conscience. James Madison, who represented a district with a strong Baptist presence, succeeded in amending Mason's language to mandate equality. As a result, the final version of the Declaration of Rights, June 12, 1776, read: "all men are equally entitled to the free exercise of religion, according to the dictates of conscience."

When the first session of Virginia's new republican government convened on October 5, it was deluged with petitions from dissenters, praying for exemption from taxes laid to support the Church of England. "These petitions," said Jefferson, who was now serving in the Virginia Assembly, "brought on the severest contest in which I have ever been engaged." A statute was passed early in December 1776, exempting dissenters from religious taxes. An exemption for Anglicans soon followed, creating a level playing field on which all were equally absolved from paying church taxes. The December act was justified, in the words of its authors, by a desire that "equal liberty, as well religious as civil, may be universally extend to all the good people of this commonwealth."

Resourceful proponents of state support for religion perceived that equality need not be their nemesis and could, in fact, be used to advance their agenda. Accordingly, they offered a proposal, called a "general assessment," which was deferred for the "Determination of a future assembly." General assessment was a simple idea: All citizens would be treated equally, each paying an equal religious tax which would be channeled to the church of his choice to pay the minister's salary or to build churches. Republican equality was now wedded to the ancient idea of coercive public support for religion.

It would be incorrect to suggest that general assessment was invented in Virginia in 1776 and copied by other states. The idea seems to have emerged spontaneously in several places. General assessment was a novelty in the religious history of the west. Professor Levy has stressed its "uniqueness" agreeing with James Madison's observation in December 1784 that "Experience gives no model of General Assessment." General assessment also changed the definition of the scholarly problem, investigated in these pages, for the state, instead of subsidizing a single church from which it expected reciprocal support, proposed, after 1776 to support all churches under its jurisdiction from whose combined beneficial influence it hoped to profit. With the advent of general assessment, the problem that interests historians and other investigators broadens from the relations between a church and the state to those between religion in general and government. Support for general assessment after 1776 can be traced from the Deep South to New England, for up and down the continent individuals thought it essential to make religion an ally, an "assistant," of their new governments. The Georgia constitution of 1777 authorized general assessment with the result that an act was passed in 1785 under the terms of which "all Christian sects and denominations were to receive tax support in proportion to the amount of property owned by their respective church members." General assessment was suggested to the drafters of the South Carolina constitution of 1778. William Tennent reported in January 1777 that "there is a proposal to establish all denominations and to pay them equally," a proposal the dissenters opposed not on principle but because they considered it to be "impracticable." The constitution, as adopted in 1778, declared the "Christian Protestant religion . . . to be the established religion of the State" and stipulated that all "Christian Protestants . . . shall enjoy equal rights and privileges." It then created a complicated system that extended the right of incorporation, previously enjoyed exclusively by the Church of England, to all Protestant churches, provided they subscribed to a set of articles beginning with a declaration "that there is one eternal God, and a future state of rewards and punishments."

In Virginia a general assessment bill was considered by the legislature in 1779; it passed a second reading in the assembly, but then stalled. Decisive action on the issue was taken in the fall of 1784, when Patrick Henry introduced in the assembly "A Bill Establishing a Provision for Teachers of the Christian Religion." Henry's bill led off with the truism that "the general diffusion of Christian knowledge hath a natural tendency to correct the morals of men, restrain their vices, and preserve the peace of society"; it then proposed a general tax that citizens could pay to the church of their choice or to a fund supporting public education. Supported by a galaxy off revolutionary heroes, including Richard Henry Lee, Edmund Pendleton, the future Chief Justice John Marshall, and George Washington, Henry's bill was approved on a first reading in the House, 47–32, and appeared to be on its way to passage. Historians have suggested that it was sidetracked in November by the elevation, contrived by Madison and others, of Henry to the governorship. Liberated from Henry's spell, the assembly voted on Christmas Eve, 1784, to submit the bill to the voters. A spirited public relations campaign turned the citizens against the general assessment bill, and it was defeated when the assembly reconvened in the fall of 1785.

The Maryland Constitution of 1776 authorized the state legislature to "lay a general and equal tax, leaving to each individual the power of appointing payment of the money, collected from him, to the support of any particular place of worship or minister." A determined attempt to implement this authority by passing a general assessment bill was mounted in 1784–5, and, as in Virginia, the effort eventually failed, although supported by the House of Representatives.

The Massachusetts Constitution of 1780 established a general assessment system by declaring that "all moneys paid by the subject to the support of public worship, and all public teachers aforesaid, shall, if he require it, be uniformly applied to the support of the public teacher or teachers of his own religious sect or denomination, provided there be any on whose instruction he attends." The administration of the program, not clearly described, was delegated, as was customary, to the state's towns, in many of which the old certificate system was grafted onto it. Interminable controversies and conflicting court decisions ensued. In two other New England states, Connecticut and Vermont (which functioned as a state until admitted to the Union in 1791), general assessment proposals were considered, but in both places and in New Hampshire as well, the familiar system of mandatory religious taxation with dissenters' exemptions, secured by certificates and other means, prevailed.

Although there was resistance to general assessment bills in every state in which they were advocated, opponents in many places left little documentation. Enough evidence survives, however, from Massachusetts and Virginia, and to a lesser degree from Maryland and Connecticut, to permit a reconstruction of the multiple arguments against government assistance to religion as they developed in the years after 1776. Had general assessment been an issue in Pennsylvania and New York, where there were lively, competitive newspapers, surviving opposition arguments would doubtless be more plentiful, but probably not different in kind from those that are available.

New England opponents of government who supported religion were a different breed from those in the South. In New England the political elites, with very few exceptions, supported the entrenched ecclesiastical system – "the most mild and equitable establishment of religion that was known in the world," said John Adams – and claimed that "the privilege of supporting public worship by law" was their "sacred right." Therefore, the articulation of the case against religious taxation fell almost exclusively to evangelical ministers, like the Baptist spokesman, Isaac Backus. The violent history of church–state relations in Virginia turned a segment of the commonwealth's political elite, foremost among whom were Jefferson and

Madison, against the Church of England and against the general assessment laws that surfaced after 1776. As a result, an alliance of convenience developed between Virginia's anticlerical politicians, many of whom were Unitarians in embryo and pietistic preachers, an alliance that existed, less conspicuously, elsewhere. The pietists and the politicians shared a common goal, the disestablishment of the "legacy" churches in their jurisdictions, but they disagreed on how far disestablishment should go and on what it actually meant. And their visions of the American religious landscape after disestablishment were very different. The politicians hoped for a republic of reason in which future generations of Americans would profess some version of "liberal" Christianity. The pietists wanted a born-again nation, convicted by the Holy Spirit and redeemed by the blood of Jesus Christ.

After 1776 four different types of argument against state-supported religion emerged: the pragmatic, the biblical, the ideological, and the legalistic. The gist of the pragmatic argument was that the history of Christianity proved that coercive government support of religion was so harmful to the morals of the clergy that it destroyed – or, at least, severely compromised – its capacity to promote the public good. It was the least compelling of the indictments of government-subsidized religion, for most Americans could see with their own eyes that government patronage had not corrupted their ministers and their churches. Congregational clergymen in New England, even their most severe critics conceded, were men of sterling character and formidable learning. By the middle of the eighteenth century, as recent scholarship has shown, Anglican clergymen were not pre-dominantly British rejects, absconding to America to booze and batten off the colonists; most of them, in Virginia and elsewhere in the south, were competent and committed native sons.

The pragmatic argument was aimed at those proponents of state support who paraded before the public the "celebrated legislators of antiquity" to bolster their case. Antiquity, their pragmatic opponents contended, taught a very different lesson about government-sponsored religion. Witness, they said, the disastrous policy of the fourth-century Roman Emperor, Constantine, in officially establishing Christianity throughout the Empire. Constantine's alleged blunder had long been a target of well-informed dissenters. In the 1640s Roger Williams asserted that the "unknowing zeal of Constantine and other emperors did more hurt to Christ Jesus' crown and kingdom than the raging fury of the most bloody Neros." In an article in the Boston *Independent Chronicle*, April 13, 1780, Philanthropos (said to have been the Boston lawyer, James Sullivan) accused Constantine of wrecking Christianity by loading "the church and the bishops with his favours" from the public treasury. As a result of the emperor's misguided policies, the "Christian religion, which for 300 years after the ascension of Jesus, had been spreading over a large part of Asia, Europe and Africa, and without the assistance of secular power and . . . was almost everywhere in a flourishing condition, in the space of another 300 years, or a little more, was greatly corrupted in a large part of that extent, its glory debased, and its light almost extinguished."

James Madison, in his Memorial and Remonstrance against Henry's bill, June 20, 1785, called attention to the baleful consequences of Constantine's action. "During almost fifteen centuries has the legal establishment of Christianity been on trial." "What," Madison asked, "have been its fruits? More or less in all places, pride and indolence in the Clergy, ignorance and servility in the laity, in both, superstition, bigotry and persecution. Enquire of the Teachers of Christianity for ages in which it appeared in its greatest lustre; those of every sect point to the ages prior to its incorporation with Civil policy." Madison's argument seeped into the most popular, evangelical petition (measured by number of signatures) against Henry's assessment bill, which informed the public in the fall of 1785 that it was not "better for the Church, when Constantine first established Christianity by human laws. True, there was rest from persecution, but how soon overrun with error, Superstition and Immorality. How unlike were Ministers then, to what they were before, both in orthodoxy of Principle and Purity of Life."

The second line of objection to coercive government support of religion, the argument from scripture, did not have roots as deep as the fourth-century Roman Empire, but it was venerable enough, stretching back to the dawn of the Reformation early in the sixteenth century. As soon as Anabaptists emerged in the 1520s, they began preaching, in opposition to both the Church of Rome and the newly established reformed churches in Germany and Switzerland, that the state must not support the church in any way, a conviction that became dogma for Baptists, Quakers, Mennonites, and other German sects who emigrated to America. Their proof text was John 18:36, the favorite of William Penn, in which Jesus Christ, in answer to Pilate's question – was he King of the Jews? – responded that "my kingdom is not of this world." To evangelicals this statement always meant that Christ's kingdom was purely spiritual and was incompatible with officially mandated material support for the church and its servants. As Virginia Presbyterians asserted on October 24, 1776, "when our Blessed Saviour declares his *kingdom is not of this world*, he renounces all dependence upon on state power." Preachers who accepted tax-generated salaries were denounced as "hirelings," "Sons of Belial," and seekers of the "fleece and not the flock." Reaching back into the Old Testament, Isaac Backus declared that "it is evident to us that God never allowed any civil state upon earth to impose religious taxes; but that he declared his vengeance against those in Israel who presumed to use force in such affairs: 1 Sam. 3:16, 34. Mic. 3:5, 12." Although Backus and many other evangelicals Christians were convinced that tax-supported religion fell under the ban of both the Old and New Testaments, they believed that there were still ways, as will presently be explained, for a government to act as the nursing father of the church. In their view John 18:36 did not trump Isaiah 49:23.

The ideological argument against tax-supported religion was grounded in a distinctive interpretative outlook, which scholars of the American Revolution began emphasizing in the 1960s. Called opposition or country ideology, this outlook is said to have exercised such a powerful grip on the revolutionary mentality that some scholars have suggested that it "caused" the American Revolution. The central feature of opposition ideology was its paranoid-like fear of power, its conviction that the principal feature of power was its "aggressiveness: its endlessly propulsive tendency to expand itself beyond legitimate boundaries" to destroy liberty. One of the main antidotes prescribed for the menace of power was jealousy, which in the eighteenth century meant suspicion, a hyperactive, deliberately cultivated suspicion that viewed power with a "watchful, hawk-eyed" vigilance, capable of detecting the first symptoms of its aggression. In his famous *Letters from a Farmer in Pennsylvania* (1768), John Dickinson had declared that "a perpetual jealousy respecting liberty is absolutely requisite in all free states." In the 1760s and 1770s, American leaders strived to cultivate "an extreme spirit of jealousy" in their fellow citizens with such conspicuous success that Charles Carroll of Maryland concluded in 1773 that "jealousy and suspicion had become the very basis of American politics."

Americans did not switch off their jealousy after 1776. They now welcomed it as a republican virtue. "Republican jealousy," they claimed, "was the guardian angel of these States." "Jealousy," observed Silas Deane in 1777, was now "the ruling feature in the American character." Americans mobilized jealousy against all manifestations of power in all arenas. The attempt to impose religious taxes in the general assessment laws was a particularly inviting target, since adepts in the art of jealousy could compare it, as Virginians did, to the Stamp Act and the Tea Act, whose trifling taxes were interpreted as being the leading edge of a deep laid conspiracy to enslave America.

Jealousy operated on the inch–mile principle: give power an inch and it would expand a mile, or, in some American imaginations, a light year. The jealous antenna of Philanthropos picked up ominous signals from the general assessment provision of the Massachusetts Constitution. "If the Legislature," he wrote in April 1780, "have a right to oblige the people to maintain teachers of piety, religion, and morality, they have also a right to define what piety, religion, and morality are, and if they have a right to define what they are, it follows that they have a right to say what the teachers shall preach to the people" and even to "establish articles of faith," deviation from which could subject dissenters to punishment. A Connecticut Baptist went even further, arguing that granting the state the power to lay religious taxes could lead, step by step, to enabling it to compel men to "worship the devil."

Madison and his fellow Virginians let their republican jealousy run to even greater lengths. In his 1785 Memorial and Remonstrance Madison saluted "prudent jealousy" as "one of the noblest characteristics of the late revolution." He then applied jealousy to the proposed Virginia general assessment act, asking "who does not see that the same authority which can establish Christianity, in exclusion of all other religions, may establish with ease any particular sect of Christians, in exclusion of all other sects." Once this abuse of power had begun, it might not end, Madison suggested later in his Memorial, until the Inquisition was established in Virginia. An auto-da-fe in Albemarle County was not, apparently, impossible. These charges were familiar – Baptists had warned that general assessment might lead to the Inquisition – and an anonymous writer in the *Virginia Gazette*, November 8, 1783, anticipated the argument in Madison's Memorial by warning that general assessment would

> certainly open a door for the great red dragon, that horrible monster persecution, to enter into our Western world. For if the legislature have a power to enforce a maintenance for the Clergy, they must also have a right to impose creeds, and forms of worship, and demand a universal conformity to them, on pain of suffering and punishment for the neglect, as they shall judge proper, both in kind and degree.

Other jealous opponents of the tax did not scruple to ensure that "the severest persecutions in England were ransacked in which to paint the burdens and scourges of religious freedom," not neglecting to speculate on the possibility of the rekindling in Virginia of the "Smithfield fires" in which Protestant martyrs had been burned alive in the 1550s.

The fourth and final argument against government-supported religion was based on a rights claim, namely, that "all men have a Naturall and Unalienable right to worship God according to the Dictates of their own Conscience and understanding." Dissenters claimed that religious taxation of any sort – even equal religious taxation of the general assessment variety – violated this right. It is important to understand what was at stake here. Proponents of tax-supporters religion maintained as stoutly as opponents that every American had a natural right to liberty of conscience, but the two camps differed, fundamentally, over the extent of that right.

The issue was this: Should freedom from religious taxation be a component of the right to liberty of conscience? Supporters of general assessment denied that it should be, for they subscribed to the inherited seventeenth-century English view, which crystallized after the passage of the Toleration Act of 1689, that liberty of conscience consisted solely in the uninhibited exercise of worship and belief. Massachusetts courts drew a distinction between "liberty of conscience and the right of appropriating money." "The former," declared Chief Justice Theophilus Parsons, "is unalienable, the latter is surrendered as the price of protection." A Boston minister, John Tucker, explained the distinction in slightly more colloquial terms in 1774. He could not see, he wrote, that religious taxes had "anything more to do with men's consciences . . . than with their coats or periwigs." General assessments taxes, Tucker continued, "should be viewed as political, not as designed to affect men's conscience, which ought always to be left to God and themselves." Religious taxes, Tucker continued, "promote the good order and welfare of the state, by making men better members of civil society." They should be regarded, therefore, as civil ordinances, just as a minister who benefited from them could be considered "a civil officer of the state." The New Hampshire Supreme Court made the distinction between government's relation to religion in its civil and spiritual dimensions clear. Wrote Chief Justice Jeremiah Smith, "public instruction in religion and morality, within the meaning of our Constitution and laws is to every purpose a civil, not a spiritual institution. The relation that subsists between a minister and the church is spiritual." Liberty of conscience was, thus, a "spiritual" matter, beyond the reach of government. Religious taxation was a "civil" matter beyond the reach of a right to liberty of conscience. Dissenters, must not, Justice Smith admonished them, mistake "their purses for their consciences."

In 1784 Virginia Presbyterians drew a distinction between the civil and spiritual sides of government support for religion. As long as the government did not encroach on "religion as a spiritual system," by which they meant "norms of worship," which were protected under liberty of conscience, it might lay religious taxes that could be considered as civil statutes. "Religion," the Presbyterians asserted, "as a Spiritual System is not to be considered as an object of human legislation; but may in a civil view, as preserving the existence & promoting the happiness of Society." It was pure demagoguery, asserted the citizens of Surry County, in November 1785, to claim that religious taxes jeopardized liberty of conscience, for under Henry's general assessment bill, "men are left as free as Air in their choice of their own religion." The distinguished Virginia jurist and commentator on Blackstone, St. George Tucker, saw in general assessment nothing "incompatible with the most perfect liberty of conscience in matters of religion."

The Massachusetts Constitution of 1780 is the primary example of an enactment of the distinction, as advocates of general assessment understood it, between the spiritual and civil spheres of religion. The "spiritual" article 2 guaranteed the right to liberty of conscience; the "civil" article 3 permitted taxation for support of religion. Like the law officers of the crown in 1732, the drafters of the constitution saw no incompatibility between the two concepts.

Dissenters certainly did, however. They complained that there was an "inconsistency," a "repugnance" between articles 2 and 3. Philanthropos claimed that articles 2 and 3 "were like a cow that gives a full pail of milk and then kicks it over." For Philanthropos and other dissenters, "a full pail of milk" was a fully expanded definition of the right to liberty of conscience. Throughout the revolutionary period, dissenters insisted that what they called "true," "full" liberty of conscience must extend beyond the bare, "British" idea of non-interference with worship and belief. It must include, they stressed, exemption from religious taxes in any form. At work here was the revolutionary dynamic, noted by numerous writers, which propelled familiar concepts beyond their accustomed boundaries into new and unanticipated areas of thought and action. Rights were particularly susceptible to this process, for, as James Wilson observed of his countrymen in 1787, "few understand the whole of these rights," and most believed that abundant "new" rights awaited discovery. It should not be surprising, then, that in many American minds the right to liberty of conscience expanded after 1776 to forbid taxation. Thus defined, the magnified right became a formidable obstacle in the path of those trying to pass general assessment acts.

The post-1776 debates in the states about general assessment laws to pay ministerial salaries focused American minds on the propriety and legality of religious taxation to the virtual exclusion of all other state–church issues. Baptists and their allies claimed that the proponents of general assessment intended to rivet new religious establishments on America, since, in their view, religious taxation was a distinguishing mark of a religious establishment. General assessment supporters assailed the "ignorance" of the Baptists "in defining religious establishment simply in terms of religious taxation." They contended that an establishment must be understood in strictly "spiritual terms." "A religious establishment by law," claimed a Boston writer in 1778, "is an establishment of a particular mode of worshipping God, with rites and ceremonies peculiar to such mode, from which the people are not suffered to vary." Courts lent their authority to this view, stating that "a religious establishment is where the state prescribes a formulary of faith and worship for the rule and government of all the subjects." Religious taxation designed to promote the public welfare, a "civil" activity, was as foreign to a definition of an establishment as it was to the meaning of liberty of conscience. The Baptists and their allies, in the view of the supporters of general assessment, were employing the revolutionary tactic of expanding the definition of an establishment beyond its traditional limits to include the imposition of nondiscriminatory religious taxes.

The dispute between the supporters and opponents of general assessment laws over the definition of an establishment of religion demonstrates that, for the Founding generation, the meaning of the term "establishment" was limited to two objectionable government actions respecting religion: the regulation of the faith and practices of its citizens and the imposition of taxes to pay preachers. There was unanimity on the first point and disagreement on the second. But, beyond these two areas, the definition of an establishment did not extend.

The controversy over general assessment was a continuation into the newly independent United States of the colonial era quarrel between members of the established churches – Congregationalist in the north, Anglican in the south – and colonial dissenters, foremost of whom were Baptists and Quakers. These last two groups had always opposed religious taxation because "it was much against Quaker and Baptist principles to request any moneys to be paid to their own Teacher as to pay another." After independence the Methodists, new on the American scene, and the Presbyterians fell in line with this view, although the approval, in Europe, of the parent bodies of both denominations of tax-supported religion, dating back in the Presbyterian case to the dawn of the Reformation, made their transition to the Baptist–Quaker position far from seamless. Methodists, who began arriving in America in small groups in the decade before the revolution, considered themselves, at first, to be a reform movement within the Church of England. In October 1776, for example, they informed the Virginia General Assembly by petition that they considered themselves to be "in communion" with the Church of England and supported her establishment in Virginia with the full panoply of powers she enjoyed in the mother country, including the power to tax all inhabitants for her support. When the Methodists became a distinctly American denomination in 1784, they ceased to advocate tax support for religion, aligning themselves with the Baptists on this point.

Between Presbyterians and Baptists and Quakers, there was settled antagonism. Charles Woodmason, a Church of England missionary working in the Carolina backcountry, noted in 1767 that the non-Anglican sects "are eternally jarring among themselves. The Presbyterians hate the Baptists far more than they do the Episcopalians." Writing in 1772, the Baptist historian, Morgan Edwards, cited instances of Presbyterians abusing Baptists in South Carolina and added that it was "remarkable that all the ill-treatment which baptists have met with in this province has come from Presbyterians." In Virginia Presbyterian ministers, disrupted Baptist services, mimicked their ministers and "slandered them to their face," denouncing their doctrines as an "awful delusion." In 1779 Presbyterians in Bedford County asked the assistance of the Hanover Presbytery in blocking the Baptists, to them "ignorant, tho' designing Sectaries," who were creating a "Dangerous Situation."

Presbyterian animosity toward the Baptists was grounded in social and theological differences, one of which was their historically conflicting positions on government assistance to religion. As heirs of Calvin, Presbyterians in Scotland and England had joined Anglicans and Congregationalists (Independents) in subscribing to the nursing father theory of the civil magistrate. In a classic of Presbyterian apologetics, *Lex Rex* (1644), Samuel Rutherford used the term "Nurse Father" to describe kings, judges, and other civil officials and explained that these worthies were not only "appointed for Civill Policy, but for the maintenance of true religion, and for the suppression of Idolatry." "The King," Rutherford declared, "hath a chiefe hand in Church affaires, when he is a Nurse-father, and beareth the Royall Sword to defend both the Tables of the Law."

Presbyterians carried the nursing father idea to America, but by 1776 differences of opinion had developed among church leaders over how far the state might go to support religion. Consequently, Presbyterians vacillated on the issue, as the general assessment contest in Virginia illustrated. Immediately after independence, Presbyterians appeared to oppose religious taxation, but when Patrick Henry introduced his general assessment bill in the assembly in the fall of 1784 the Hanover Presbytery rallied to his support, asserting in a petition of November 12, 1784, that since it was "absolutely necessary to the existence & welfare of every political combination of men to have the support of religion," religion should be subsidized by the state. In April 1785 Madison denounced the proassessment Presbyterians as being "as ready to set up an establishment which is to take them in as they were to pull down that which shut them out." Most Presbyterians moved back to the Madisonian position in the final stages of the struggle against general assessment.

If a consensus developed among Baptists, Methodists, and Presbyterians that religious taxes were inadmissable in the American republic, there was also a consensus among these three major evangelical groups and most of the minor ones in the new republic that there were many ways in which the country's "political fathers" could assist the nation's churches. After independence Baptists and other dissenters were not doctrinaire separationists on the question of government aid to religion. They tended to adopt a "live and let live" attitude. Baptists at the Massachusetts Constitutional Convention of 1780 took the position that, if any group wanted to support their own ministers with taxes, "they for their part did not wish to deprive any such ... provided those of a contrary sentiment might be at full liberty to support public worship voluntarily." In Maryland Baptists and their allies circulated a petition in March 1785 that stated that "if any church wishes for a law to compel their own society to pay, others cannot object to that measure; but why should those who do not desire, or make a conscience of doing it, be forced by law?" Dissenters were, in fact, pleased to accept what a Baptist spokesman called the government's "friendly aids to the cause of our holy religion."

The list of those "friendly aids" was long. At least one of them – incorporation – employed the coercive power of the state on behalf of Baptists and other groups who denounced that power when it took the form of taxation. Beginning in the 1790s, states began passing general incorporation acts, which permitted churches routinely to form corporations, investing them with the powers of banks, canal companies, or other businesses. Using their corporate status, churches could sue delinquent members to collect their pledges in civil courts and rely on sheriffs and constables to obtain the monies owed them. A disillusioned Baptist complained that he knew of congregations in his denomination in which "cattle and horses were taken by force [i.e., legal distraint upon court orders] to pay baptist ministers for preaching." Incorporation was especially popular with Baptists in eastern Massachusetts and in South Carolina. In 1791 it was enthusiastically adopted in Pennsylvania, a place where state coercion in religion had been abhorred during the colonial period. It spread throughout the country in the nineteenth century. To critics, incorporation resulted in a backdoor establishment of religion, every bit as objectionable as the prewar Anglican and Congregational regimes.

A scholarly expert contends that most former dissenters, including Baptists, also supported state coercion in the form of compulsory church attendance laws. All evangelical and pietistic groups believed that state governments could and should pass laws to protect the sanctity of the Christian Sabbath, proscribing work, travel, and the like on that holy day. Overwhelming numbers of dissenters approved of the "inculcation of religion in the public schools." Virtually no one objected to the state's "legislating morality" by criminalizing conduct forbidden in the Old and New Testaments. Here Pennsylvania and Rhode Island stood shoulder to shoulder with Massachusetts and Connecticut, for William Penn and Roger Williams believed as fervently as did John Winthrop in God's covenant with society, which required obedience to the divine statutes and ordinances. "Wildness and Loosesness of the People provoke the Indignation of God against a Country," Penn declared in his famous *Frame of Government* (1682); accordingly, he required his magistrates to repress an encyclopedic list of moral offenses, including everything from "Prophane Talking" to "Whoredom" to "Stage Plays" to cock-fighting. Penn's successors and magistrates in other colonies without established churches adhered to these policies up to and beyond independence. Most dissenters except Quakers and related German sects were prepared to grant to the state the power to impose test oaths on public officials. Pennsylvania, Delaware, and New Jersey, all dissenting strongholds before 1776, adopted republican constitutions in 1776. The first two authorized test oaths that limited public office to Christians, the third to Protestants. Only two states – New York and Virginia – which adopted republican constitutions between 1776 and 1787 refrained from permitting the state to impose test oaths. Virtually all dissenters believed that the state should have the power to punish blasphemy. After 1776, twelve of the thirteen states had a blasphemy law, which, as Professor Levy has reminded us, "protects and favors Christianity over other religions." I have been unable to find a single dissenter who objected to the practice, widespread before and after 1776, of governments at all levels putting public space at the disposal of religious groups for the conduct of church services. The militant Baptist leader, John Leyland, friend of Jefferson and Madison, boasted late in life that he had preached in "thirty-seven court houses [and] several capitols." None of his fellow Baptists were bashful about preaching Christ on public property.

These "friendly aids," proffered by the state, were welcomed by dissenters as signs of the "sweet harmony" (Isaac Backus's term), which they believed should prevail between government and religion. Although their sweet harmony was not flavored with the strong dollop of religious taxation favored by the general assessment proponents, the dissenters cherished it as much as their adversaries and were not, in fact, prepared to concede to them the powerful nursing father metaphor, which historically had been as much the property of evangelical Christians as of their opponents.

George Whitefield, had used the metaphor in a sermon before a huge crowd in Philadelphia in 1746. The New Light Congregationalist leader, Isaac Holly, glossed it in a 1765 sermon in the following way: "when Men are in the Enjoyment of this Liberty [of conscience], by civil Authority, then Kings may become Nursing fathers, and Queens Nursing Mothers to the Church of God." In 1773 Isaac Backus told his fellow New Englanders that the "promise that kings shall become nursing fathers and queens nursing mothers carries in its very nature an impartial care and tenderness for all their children." In a memorial to the Massachusetts Provincial Congress, December 2, 1774, the Baptists urged that "civil rulers ought undoubtedly to be nursing fathers to the church, by reproof, exhortation, and their own good and liberal example, as well as to protect and defend her against justice and oppression." Finally, in 1788, Presbyterians, meeting in Philadelphia, revised the denomination's 1729 confession to include the following addition to the main text: "as nursing fathers it is the duty of civil magistrates to protect the Church of our common Lord, without giving preference to any denomination of Christians above the rest."

One of the questions overlooked by scholars making generalizations about the new republic's views on the relationship between government and religion is this: Who assisted the dissenters in defeating general assessment in Virginia and Maryland and in almost defeating it in Massachusetts? The defeat of general assessment in Virginia required far more manpower than the Baptists – no more than 10 percent of the population in 1772 – and other dissenters could muster. Similarly, in Massachusetts, Baptists comprised less than 5 percent of the population in 1774, yet more than 40 percent of the voters opposed Article 3 of the 1780 Constitution, which

authorized general assessment. Who were the nondissenting opponents in both states? General assessment supporters reviled them
as atheists, infidels, freethinkers, freeloaders, and malcontents of
every sort. But these libels do not change the reality that many of
the opponents were distinguished citizens whose only vice was that
of changing their minds.

George Washington, for example, supported general assessment
until he saw that the controversy it generated was rending Virginia's
social fabric. By October 1785 he concluded that dropping the measure would be "productive of more quiet to the State, than by enacting
it into a Law: which, in my opinion, wou'd be impolitic, admitting
there is a decided majority for it, to the disgust of a respectable majority." A similar situation occurred in Maryland. General assessment
there was supported by Samuel Chase, William Paca, and other well-
known patriots, but, according to George Lux, efforts to pass the measure "convulsed" the state, arousing opponents to swear that "they
would fight it to the last drop of their blood." To preserve political
peace, proponents of general assessment, who, Lux claimed, commanded a two-thirds majority in the House of Representatives and
outnumbered opponents seven to five throughout the state, ceased to
support the measure, allowing the opposition to defeat it. A similar
dynamic was at work in Massachusetts, where Congregationalists
voted in numbers against general assessment in the interest of preserving comity in their communities.

Historians have a name – "politiques" – for those leaders
and followers who value social harmony above religious agendas.
Elizabeth I, described as a "politique" leader, was determined to
prevent private beliefs, however "scriptural," from condensing into
rival religious groups, who would disturb the public peace; she
prized social and political stability above religious correctness.

Historians have identified other distinguished politiques among Elizabeth's contemporaries: Catherine d'Medici, William the Silent, Wallenstein. After 1776 many Americans, from Washington on down, adopted a politique attitude toward religious questions, a posture that complicates the task of scholars, who must decide, in many cases, the extent to which public positions and policies represent the true convictions of the actor.

Even though the relationship of government to religion in the early republic may seem to be complex, it is easier to understand than the situation in England in July 1661, when Charles II told his parliament that "those [questions] which concern religion, I confess to you, are too hard for me." It is possible to offer confident judgments about where the nation stood in 1787, on the eve of the Constitutional Convention. On one subject there was unanimity: Governments must not interfere in the spiritual realm of religion, in men's beliefs and modes of worship. It must forever renounce the polices of the dark ages of the doctrine of exclusive salvation in which a state imposed on its population what it regarded as true faith and practice, dissent from which was criminal. Everyone agreed that the spiritual realm must be walled off from government.

Beyond this wall disagreement reigned. Most Americans, who were members of churches established in the colonial era, believed that as long as government treated its citizens equally, it could, acting as a nursing father, tax them to support churches and exercise other coercive powers on religion's behalf. Many other Americans, predominately dissenters during the colonial period, passionately disagreed with this position. They would have built another wall, parallel to the first, which would have shielded religion from taxation, even if imposed equally and with the intention of producing "civil" good. But beyond this second wall, these former dissenters discerned areas in which government, acting as a more restrained nursing father, could assist religion. For some these areas were large; for others small, but few could be found, as the delegates assembled in Philadelphia in May 1787, who would have totally renounced what the Baptist preacher called friendly aids to the church. A large majority of Americans believed, in short, that some connection between government and religion was not only possible but desirable.

4

The Constitution and Beyond

NEITHER THE REVOLUTIONARY STATE GOVERNMENTS nor the Articles of Confederation gave Americans a stable, prosperous society. Consequently, a group of energetic, young leaders, responding to a demand (that they themselves had helped stimulate) for a new national government, convened in Philadelphia in May 1787 and in four months produced the federal Constitution, the *summa* of American statecraft.

Critics attacked the Constitution from all angles as soon as its text became public in mid-September. Believers accused the Framers of selling out the nation's faithful by showing "cold indifference towards religion." To other distressed churchgoers it appeared that "in all probability the composers had no thought of God in all their consultations." Some accused the Framers of recklessly repudiating America's covenant with God; "if civil rulers won't acknowledge God, he won't acknowledge them; and they must perish from the way." These kinds of complaints continued to dog the Constitution. In 1789 Benjamin Rush informed John Adams that "many pious people wish the name of the Supreme Being had been introduced somewhere in the new Constitution." A few years later, Timothy Dwight still could not conceal his unhappiness: "we found the Constitution without any acknowledgement of God; without any recognition of his mercies to us . . . or even of his existence. The Convention, by which it was formed, never asked, even once, his direction or his blessing upon their labours."

The Constitution did, in fact, glance in the Almighty's direction – certifying in Article 7 that it was adopted "in the Year of our Lord" 1787 and recognizing, in Article 1, Section 7, the sanctity of the Sabbath by excluding it from the ten days in which a president was obliged to return a bill to Congress. In three places the Constitution required officials to take an oath, which commentators have judged to be "a religious act." As James Iredell explained in the North Carolina Ratifying Convention, "according to the modern definition of an oath, it is considered a solemn appeal to the Supreme Being, for the truth of what is said, by a person who believes in the existence of a Supreme Being and in a future state of rewards and punishments." If these actions were efforts to smuggle religion into the Constitution, they did not appease pious Americans who considered them proof enough that the Framers had unaccountably turned their backs on God.

Partisans in the late twentieth-century disputes about the relationship between government and religion have used the complaints of the disillusioned believers, just quoted, and other similar ones to prove that the Framers deliberately wrote a "Godless Constitution." This phrase has a certain shock value – as those who coined it intended – because the Framers were not "godless" men. How, then, could they have written a "godless" Constitution?

During the Revolutionary War many Framers had drafted proclamations in state legislatures and in Congress beseeching God to intervene on their country's behalf and many, at the state and local level, had favored government support of religious institutions. Even some of the rationally inclined Framers were convinced that they and their colleagues had received divine assistance at Philadelphia. Benjamin Franklin said that he had

> so much faith in the general Government of the world by Providence, that I can hardly conceive a Transaction of such momentous Importance to the Welfare of Millions now existing, and to exist in the Posterity of a great nation, should be suffered to pass without being in some degree influenc'd, guided, and governed by that omnipotent, omnipresent, and beneficent Ruler in whom all inferior Spirits live, and move, and have their Being.

In *Federalist* 37 Madison wrote that "it is impossible for the man of pious reflection not to perceive in it [the Constitution] a finger of that Almighty hand which has been so frequently and signally extended to our relief in the critical stages of the revolution." Finally, Washington wrote of tracing, "with a kind of grateful and pious exaltation . . . the finger of Providence through those dark and mysterious events, which first induced the states to appoint a general Convention and then led them one after another . . . into an adoption of the system recommended by that general Convention."

These pious effusions do not, however, conceal the fact that the Constitution is a secular document. It contains no conspicuous acknowledgment of God nor does it attempt to incorporate religion into the structure or operations of government. Men who respected God had apparently written, as charged, a "godless" document. Why?

In a speech to the convention on June 28, Benjamin Franklin offered a clue about the fortunes of religion at Philadelphia. Franklin reproved his fellow delegates for forgetting God, that "powerful Friend," who guided America to victory over the mighty British Empire. I have lived "a long time," Franklin explained, "and the longer I live, the more convincing proofs I see of this Truth – *that God governs in the Affairs of Men....* We have been assured, Sir, in the Sacred Writings, that 'except the Lord build the House, they labour in vain that build it.' I firmly believe this; and I also believe, that, without his concurring Aid, we shall succeed in this political Building no better than the Builders of babel." Accordingly, Franklin moved that "prayers, imploring the Assistance of Heaven, and its Blessing on our Deliberations, be held in this Assembly every morning." The motion failed, ostensibly because the convention lacked funds to pay local clergymen to act as chaplains.

The delegates, Franklin scolded, needed to remember what they had done at the First Continental Congress: "in the beginning of the Contest with G. Britain, when we were sensible of danger we had daily prayers in this room for divine protection." What Franklin meant was that in 1774 war was imminent – just after the First Congress convened, reports swept Philadelphia that the British navy had bombarded Boston – and from that moment to at least 1782 every member of Congress – every state and local official for that matter – was in personal peril. A sudden shift in the fortunes of war might bring everyone to the gallows as traitors. Consequently, the First and subsequent Congresses were composed of anxious men who packed official pronouncements with religious language.

Members of the Constitutional Convention felt that they too were meeting in a time of national crisis, but many of their fellow citizens disagreed, accusing them of exaggerating the nation's problems so that they could personally profit from a new political order of their own devising. If there was, in fact, a genuine crisis in 1787, it was a different kind of predicament from the one the nation faced in 1774. No one's life was in danger. The issues before the convention were not matters of war and peace but complicated problems in political science such as the empowerment of a national government, representation in a bicameral legislature, and the establishment of a republican executive. Although the convention delegates believed that nothing escaped the notice of God, they evidently considered it unseemly to request divine assistance for problems best solved by bargaining between political power brokers.

A more compelling reason why religion was absent from the Constitution was that its inclusion would have been fatal to the plans of the Framers. Many of them concluded that the common denominator running through the troubles that brought them to Philadelphia – social instability, unjust legislative majorities, economic distress – was the irresponsible civic behavior of the body politic. James Wilson spoke for the Framers when he complained in 1787 that "the rock of Freedom, which stood firm against the attacks of a foreign foe, has been sapped and undermined by the licentiousness of our own citizens." There was a remedy for popular licentiousness: the improvement of national morality by strengthening the forces of religion with financial subsidies, funded by general assessments or other forms of taxation, laid by the national or state governments. During the Confederation period, general assessment proposals had caused political discord wherever proposed, terrifying a segment of the population with visions of the red dragon of persecution and with inquisitors poised to put dissenters to the torch. The prospect of religious taxation had manifestly disturbed the "public Quiet," as Washington and Madison both asserted 1785.

In 1798 John Adams experienced how inflammatory the exercise of a familiar religious act by a national official could be in a country that had been taught to cultivate and cherish republican jealousy. On March 23 of that year, when the nation was in the midst of a "quasi-war" with France, Adams proclaimed a national day of fasting and humiliation, a practice that American magistrates had followed since the earliest days of the seventeenth century. It so happened that the General Assembly of the Presbyterian Church was meeting in Philadelphia when Adams issued his proclamation. Though not a Presbyterian, Adams was branded one by his political opponents and was accused of scheming to rivet a Presbyterian establishment on the nation, the evidence being his fast day proclamation. "A general suspicion prevailed," he wrote, "that the Presbyterian Church was ambitious and aimed at an establishment as a national church. I was represented as a Presbyterian and at the head of this political and ecclesiastical project." The result of his fast day proclamation, Adams claimed, was his defeat in the presidential election of 1800. The lesson, he said, "was that nothing is more dreaded than the national government meddling with religion."

The delegates to the Philadelphia Convention were aware of this dread. Washington, Hamilton, and other like-minded delegates, who in principle had no objections to funding and employing religion to produce virtuous citizens, were certain that injecting religion in any form into the Constitution would antagonize voters who might already be dubious about the document for other reasons. Religion, therefore, was banished from the Constitution for political considerations not because of any generalized enmity to it. It is, accordingly, more appropriate to speak of a politique Constitution than a "Godless" one.

As the advocates of the "Godless" Constitution freely acknowledge, religion was not, in fact, completely banished from the Constitution, for the document, as adopted by the delegates on September 17, 1787, contained in Article VI, clause 3, a ban on religious tests "as a Qualification to any Office or public trust under the United States." The author of the test ban was Charles Pinckney of South Carolina, who told his fellow delegates that "the prevention of

Religious tests . . . is a provision the world will expect from you, in the establishment of a System founded on Republican Principles, in an age so liberal and enlightened as the present." Pinckney's proposal passed "by a great majority," although an undetermined number of delegates supported test oaths. According to Luther Martin of Maryland, "there were some members [himself included] so unfashionable as to think, that a belief in the existence of a Deity, and of a state of future rewards and punishments would be some security for the good conduct of our rulers, and that, in a Christian country, it would be at least decent to hold out some distinction between professors of Christianity and downright infidels."

After the Constitution became public, substantial numbers of Baptists supported Martin's view that the federal government must have the power to impose religious test oaths, although some Baptist leaders, including Backus and Leland, disagreed with their brethren on the issue. Baptists and other like-minded people convinced themselves that, if the federal government were divested of its power to administer religious tests to public officials Catholics, Jews, "pagans, deists, and Mahometans might obtain offices among us." To some, it was not inconceivable that the Pope might become president. And, if a Jew became chief executive, "our dear posterity may be ordered to rebuild Jerusalem." A North Carolina Baptist minister warned that "the exclusion of religious tests is by many thought dangerous and impolitic." The votaries of "Jupiter, Juno, Minerva, Proserpine, or Pluto" might infiltrate American governments. "We ought," the minister continued, to "be suspicious of our liberties. We have felt the effects of oppressive measures, and know the happy consequences of being jealous of our rights."

As the Constitution emerged from the convention on September 17, 1787, it was, despite its ban on religious tests and its furtive glances at God, a secular document. But so was the Articles of

Confederation, whose text, aside from prescribing an oath for commissioners settling boundary disputes, said nothing about God or religion. The drafters of both documents gave the federal government no power to inject itself into the religious sphere. Both assumed that whatever meaningful interaction occurred between government and religion would take place at the state level. The unamended Constitution, in short, left the relationship between religion and government exactly as it found it under the Articles of Confederation. And, as will appear, officials acting under the Constitution, assumed, as their predecessors acting under the Articles had done, that they possessed certain undefined powers to act in religious matters that would be acceptable to their constituents.

The fear of the Pope and the minions of Minerva and Pluto was symptomatic of a much broader jealousy that consumed the opponents of the new Constitution, who were soon labeled Antifederalists, to them an unfair and distasteful epithet. To Madison and his fellow Framers, the Antifederalists had let their jealousy run wild. In *Federalist* 46 Madison commended their "sober apprehensions of genuine patriotism" but assailed them for surrendering themselves to the "incoherent dreams of a delirious jealousy." Returning to the subject in *Federalist* 55, Madison railed against the Antifederalists' eagerness "to renounce every rule by which events are to be calculated, and to substitute an indiscriminate and unbounded jealousy with which all reasoning must be in vain."

Jealousy convinced many Antifederalists that the Constitutional Convention was "as deep and wicked a conspiracy as ever was invented in the darkest ages against the liberties of a free people." The intention of the Framers, they believed, was to deprive Americans of their liberties, to bring to fruition an "insidious and long meditated design of enslaving their fellow citizens." From one end of the continent to the other, Antifederalists charged that there was a conspiracy afoot to degrade Americans from "respectable, independent citizens, to abject, dependent . . . slaves." The Framers would accomplish this nefarious objective, Antifederalists believed, by putting into operation the oppressive, "consolidated" government they had designed at Philadephia, one that would emasculate the individual states and prevent them from protecting the people's liberties.

Was there any language in the new Constitution, the Antifederalists anxiously asked, that protected religious liberty? No, there was not a word. State bills of rights guarded liberty of conscience. But the Constitution that emerged from the Philadelphia convention contained no bill of rights. There must, the Antifederalists insisted, be a bill of rights in the new Constitution that would conserve liberty of conscience as well as other fundamental rights of the people.

Leaders of the Federalists, as supporters of the new Constitution were called, received these suggestions with impatience and, in some cases, with indignation. They believed that a bill of rights was unnecessary, dangerous and ineffective, and that its high-profile supporters were insincere and malicious. Bills of rights, the Federalists held, were unnecessary because the Framers had given the new government no power to touch religion. "Why," Alexander Hamilton wrote in a characteristic rejoinder to the Antifederalists, "declare that things shall not be done which there is no power to do." Bills of rights were dangerous because by singling out a few rights for protection, they might be interpreted to mean that all other rights were ceded to the government. They were ineffective, wrote Madison to Jefferson on October 17, 1788, because "experience proves the inefficacy of a bill of rights on those occasions when its control is most needed. . . . Repeated violations of these parchment barriers have been committed by overbearing majorities in every State." Finally, the Federalists were convinced – and most modern historians agree with them – that Antifederalist leaders concocted the bill of rights issue to inflame the population against the Constitution, not because they were truly worried about the danger to their fellow citizens' liberties but because they wanted to gut the Constitution to preserve the power of the state governments in which they had invested their careers.

Federalist arguments did not blunt the demand for a bill of rights, which became "the favorite topics of the ablest Antifederal declaimers." Beginning with the ratification contest in Massachusetts in February 1788, the Federalists were obliged to promise, as the price of approval of the Constitution by the state conventions, that they would seek to amend it as soon as the new government was up and running. In Virginia there was high anxiety about the Constitution's apparent indifference to religious liberty. On March 7, 1788, for example, the Virginia General Baptist Committee unanimously resolved that the Constitution failed to make "sufficient provision for the secure enjoyment of religious liberty." Simultaneously, a memorandum was placed in Madison's hands from his friend, the influential Baptist leader John Leland, in which Leland asserted that "what is dearest of all – *Religious Liberty* – is not secured." Fearing, evidently, that the Constitution might pave the way for a return to the pre-1776 regime of government-established religion in Virginia, Leland worried that "if a Majority of Congress with the President favour one system more than another, they may oblige all others to pay to support their system as much as they please."

At the Virginia Ratifying Convention, which met in June 1788, Madison did not conceal his conviction that a bill of rights was not needed to protect religious liberty. Employing his pet theory about the public benefits of a plurality of groups, Madison asserted on June 12 that a "multiplicity of sects . . . is the best and only security for religious liberty in any society. For where there is such a variety of sects, there cannot be a majority of any one sect to oppress and persecute the rest." Madison, nevertheless, supported the Federalist strategy of promising to amend the Constitution when the new government went into operation. The Virginia Convention ratified the Constitution, 89–79, and recommended forty amendments.

Madison's work at the Virginia Ratifying Convention did not neutralize the religious liberty issue. Running for a seat in the First Federal Congress in the winter of 1789 in a district that had been gerrymandered by Patrick Henry to include hosts of Antifederalists, Madison found himself confronted by a rumor, spread by opponents, that "he had ceased to be a friend to the rights of conscience." He refuted this calumny in public letters to various constituents, promising, if elected, to work for amendments protecting religious liberty. Madison defeated James Monroe in a close race and took his seat in the First Congress, sitting in New York, on March 14, 1789.

"Bound in honor and duty" to his constituents to amend the Constitution, Madison lobbied his colleagues to take action as soon as possible, making something of a nuisance of himself to men like Senator Ralph Izard of South Carolina, who hoped "we shall not be wasting time with idle discussions about amendments of the Constitution; but that we shall go to work immediately about the Finances, & endeavour to extricate ourselves from our present embarrassed & disgraceful situation." Privately, Madison indicated that he shared Izard's distaste for the amending initiative, informing Jefferson on March 29, 1789, that "conciliating" amendments would have to offered "to extinguish opposition to the system, or at least break the force of it, by detaching the deluded opponents from their designing leaders." In August Madison went further, complaining to a friend about the "nauseous project of amendments" that was taking so much of his time. In public Madison took a different tone, acknowledging the sincerity of the ordinary Antifederalists' anxieties about a possible erosion of their rights and conceding that many of their leaders were "respectable for their talents, their patriotism, and respectable for the jealousy they have for their liberty, which, though mistaken in its object is laudable in its motive."

On May 4 Madison moved that the House of Representatives "debate the subject of Amendments to the Constitution." Action was postponed until June 8, when Madison, at last, introduced his "long expected amendments." In analyzing Madison's amendments and describing how they fared in Congress, it is essential to keep in mind that the evidence available to reconstruct their passage through the House and Senate is so woeful that a conscientious historian must admit that his account is, in many instances, little better than guesswork. For the First Congress the Journals of the House and Senate are merely registers of motions made by the members. They contain no floor debates nor any information about deliberations in committees. Such debates as are available were published by shorthand reporters, whose techniques were "like all 'eighteenth century shorthand . . . inadequate to the task of recording speeches verbatim.'" The principal shorthand reporter, Thomas Lloyd, published the House debates (the Senate barred reporters) in a volume that he called the *Congressional Register*. Reprinted in 1834, as the *Annals of Congress*, it is the principal source of documentation for the evolution and adoption of the Bill of Rights. Lloyd's shorthand records have been deciphered by a modern specialist who has demonstrated that what he published about the Bill of Rights "bears only a slight resemblance to the literal transcription of his own notes. Sometimes a speech is printed for which no notes or only very brief notes exist; sometimes a long speech reported in the manuscript is printed briefly or not at all. "Lloyd's notes are interrupted by doodling, a mark of a mind wandering, caused, no doubt, by the excessive drinking in which he indulged in 1789. It is no wonder that on May 9, 1789, Madison condemned Lloyd's *Congressional Register* for exhibiting "the strongest evidences of perversion & mutilation" and Elbridge Gerry complained that "sometimes members were introduced as uttering arguments directly the reverse of what they had advanced." Such is the nature of the "evidence" from which an account of the origins of the Bill of Rights must be written.

We must also remember that, instead of packaging his amendments and placing them at the end of the Constitution, as was done in August at the suggestion of Roger Sherman, creating the Bill of Rights in the form we now know it, Madison incorporated his June 8 amendments into the body of the Constitution. Article I, section 9, of the Constitution contains a list of actions that Congress is forbidden to take (i.e., suspending the writ of habeas corpus, passing ex post facto laws). Madison proposed to increase the number of prohibited Congressional actions by inserting in section 9 the following language: the "civil rights of none shall be abridged on account of religious belief or worship, nor shall any national religion be established, nor shall the full and equal rights of conscience be in any manner, or on any pretext infringed." Madison did not stop here, however. In Article I, section 10, which contains a list of actions that the states are forbidden to take (i.e., emitting bills of credit, impairing the obligations of contracts), Madison proposed to insert this phrase: "No state shall violate the equal rights of commerce."

None of the amendments Madison offered on June 8 were "structural" – those that would have tilted the balance of power back toward the state governments by limiting the national government's authority to tax, by inhibiting its ability to employ military force, or by restricting the jurisdiction of the federal judiciary – all favorites of Antifederalist leaders. Madison's amendments protected civil and religious liberties, which the Federalists denied were endangered. Hence, they appeared to his fellow Federalists as inconsequential and were roundly ridiculed as "milk-and-water amendments," "bread pills" for an imaginary illness, "a little Flourish and Dressing." Madison, in short, was viewed as having cobbled together a string of libertarians platitudes, designed to please the witless Antifederalist multitude – as having cleverly thrown a "tub to the whale," as sailors did to divert sea creatures who menaced their ships.

Madison, however, had prepared his amendment with care and calculation, According to the cynical Massachusetts congressman, Fisher Ames, his amendments "were the fruit of much labour and research," which would not have surprised anyone familiar with Madison's indefatigable industry in mastering every aspect of American statecraft. Madison, Ames claimed, had "hunted up all the grievances and complaints of newspapers – all the articles of Conventions – and the small talk of their debates." "Upon the whole," Ames concluded, Madison's amendments "may do good towards quieting men who attend to sounds only, and may get the mover some popularity – which he wishes."

What did Madison learn from his research into the nearly two hundred amendments suggested by the state ratifying conventions? He learned that some of the ratifying states concluded that the Constitution posed no danger to religion. The amendments offered by Massachusetts and South Carolina did not mention religion. Nor did Maryland's amendments, although the state constitutional convention rejected a proposal that "there be no national religion established by law; but that all persons be equally entitled to protection in their religious liberty" (there is no evidence, however, that the delegates who turned down this resolution favored the establishment of a "national religion.")

The Pennsylvania Convention recommended no amendments. The state's Antifederalist minority, however, adopted an unofficial "Dissent" on December 18, 1787, stating that "the rights of conscience shall be held inviolable: and neither the legislative, executive, nor the judicial powers of the United States shall have authority to alter, abrogate, or infringe any part of the constitution of the several states, which provide for the preservation of liberty in matters of religion." New Hampshire wanted assurances that Congress could make "no Laws touching Religion" nor exercise powers to "infringe the rights of Conscience." The three states in which the passage of the Constitution encountered the roughest passage – Virginia, New York, and North Carolina (which did not ratify until 1789) – recommended in common the amendments proposed by Virginia, which stated that "all men have an equal, natural and unalienable right to the free exercise of religion according to the dictates of conscience, and that no particular religious sect or society ought to be favored or established by Law in preference to others." Nowhere, not in the invectives of mudslingers abusing each other in the nation's newspapers nor in the more decorous debates in the state ratifying conventions, did Madison encounter a demand for the separation of church and state.

Madison discovered that in 1789 in many parts of the nation the division persisted over the issue that had convulsed Virginia in 1784–5: Were religious denominations to be funded by public taxation or were they to be left "to shift for themselves" by relying on voluntary contributions? This issue continued to elicit competing definitions of liberty of conscience and of the scope of religious establishments. Most of the Federalists had been allied with or were in sympathy with the established churches of the colonial era; they subscribed to the limited, "spiritual" conception of liberty of conscience and of a religious establishment, contending that both were confined to religious faith and practice and that religious taxation was an unrelated "civil" matter, outside the orbit of both. The Antifederalists were principally members of colonial dissenting sects, Baptists, and others, who took a more expansive view of liberty of conscience and religious establishments, insisting that both comprehended religious taxation and that both could be invoked to forbid it. In presenting "religious" amendments to the Constitution, Madison saw his task as the delicate one of placating the Antifederalists without offending the Federalists, thus securing the support of both groups for the Constitution. He knew that, in formulating amendments, he must address their different understandings of the liberty of conscience and religious establishments. His challenge was to craft language that would simultaneously satisfy holders of strongly held, conflicting views on these matters.

Madison's strategy was to resolve these problems within the context of small f federalism, which received its classic expression in the Tenth Amendment to the Constitution: "the powers not delegated to the United States by the Constitution, nor prohibited by it to the States, are reserved to the States respectively, or to the people." Here, in Madison's and many of his fellow Federalists' view, was the articulation of the theory of the Constitution that the jealous Antifederalists had been unable or unwilling to comprehend. And here, of course, was the reason the Federalists insisted that amendments to protect religion against the national government were unnecessary – Congress had no power to legislate on religion. As Madison declared at the Virginia Ratifying Convention: "there is not a shadow of right in the General Government to intermeddle with religion. Its least interference with it would be a most flagrant usurpation." At one point Jefferson suggested that the Tenth Amendment alone might be sufficient to quit the anxieties of religious dissenters, but Madison knew that the jealousy of his constituents in Virginia would not be assuaged unless guarantees against religious oppression were explicitly spelled out.

Comparing the respective limitations on the powers of Congress and the state governments in Madison's inserted phrases in Article I, sections 9 and 10, reveals how he tilted his amendments toward federalism. In Article I, section 9, he forbade Congress to establish a "national religion." In Article I, section 10, an establishment of religion is not mentioned, which meant, presumably, that as odious as the prospect would have been for Madison, section 10 did not preclude a state establishment. In section 9 Madison specified that Congress not infringe the "full" rights of conscience, using the expansive adjective which would have been universally understood to mean that Congress was prevented from laying religious taxes, including those of the "nonpreferential" kind, which general assessment laws levied. In section 10, on the other hand, Madison used the old, limited definition of liberty of conscience (omitting "full"), which permitted states to lay religious taxes, without being accused of violating consciences. His amendments vested the states with substantial powers in the religious realm, which the national government did not have. Madison must have expected to satisfy the Antifederalists, by explicitly stripping the national government of intrusive power in religious matters, and the Federalists, especially those in New England, by maintaining considerable state autonomy in religion.

The issue of state autonomy arose in mid-August, generating the only discussion in the First Congress about the religious amendments which the shorthand reporters captured and preserved. On July 28 the House received a report from a select committee, which recommended revising Madison's amendments so that the insertion in Article I, section 9, read: "no religion shall be established by law." Dropped was Madison's modifier "national," which alarmed the New England delegates who feared eliminating a word that limited Congress's involvement with religion to the "national" level might suggest that it could "intermeddle" with religion in the states.

If the report in the *Congressional Register* of a House debate of August 15 can be trusted, Benjamin Huntington of Connecticut made a remarkably prescient analysis of the problem the language of the revised amendment posed for New England. Huntington told Madison that "he understood the amendment to mean what had been expressed" by him [Madison] but that "others might find it convenient to put another construction upon it." What troubled Huntington was that, because preachers' salaries and church construction in the states "to the eastward" [New England] were funded by public taxes, "'if an action was brought before a federal court on any of these cases, the person who neglected to perform his engagements could not be compelled to do it; for a support of ministers, or building of places of might be construed into a religious establishment." Huntington feared that the national government, through the agency of its courts, might find a way to arrogate to itself power over religion in New England and, using an expansive definition of a religious establishment, terminate the region's time-honored practice of supporting religion with public taxation.

What Huntington feared actually happened in 1940, when the Supreme Court, under its theory of incorporation, decided that the

language of the First Amendment, prohibiting Congress from making laws establishing a religion, applied to the states and brought
their religious practices under the scrutiny of the federal courts. To
put Huntington and his fellow New Englanders at ease, Madison
declared that "if the word national was inserted before religion,"
making the amendment read "no national religion shall be established by law," "it would satisfy the minds of the honorable gentlemen." And, in fact, Madison moved in Congress that very day to
restore to the amendment the word "national." His objective was to
make it clear that restraint on Congress's authority over religion at
the national level could not be construed to authorize interference
with religion elsewhere. Religion in the states must be kept beyond
the reach of any agency of the national government. Federalism must
not be compromised, even if it protected the levying of religious taxes
at the state level.

On August 24 the House agreed to seventeen amendments, enu-
merated as Articles I through XVII, which it now proposed to add
seriatim at the end of the Constitution and sent them to the Senate.
Article III of the seventeen was the old, amended Article I, section 9. It now read: "Congress shall make no law establishing religion or prohibiting the free exercise thereof, nor shall the rights of
Conscience be infringed." New England continued to object to the
language of Article III, despite Roger Sherman's appeal to his countrymen to stop worrying about words relating to religion, "inasmuch
as congress had no authority whatever delegated to them by the
constitution, to make religious establishments." On September 9
Senator Oliver Ellsworth of Connecticut, like Sherman a Framer of
the Constitution, persuaded the Senate to substitute in Article III the
phrase "articles of faith or a mode of worship" for the word "religion."
Article III now read "Congress shall make no law establishing

articles of faith, or a mode of worship, or prohibiting the free exercise of religion." What Ellsworth had done was to insert the limited, "spiritual," definition of liberty of conscience, which permitted religious taxation, in the proposed Bill of Rights, and to eliminate any reference to a "religious establishment" which might lend itself, in the hands of an unfriendly court, to a broad construction, incompatible with publicly supported religion in New England.

The Senate's amendments were read in the House on September 14, which refused to accept Ellsworth's version of Article III, apparently because the members realized that his stripping out of the amendment any specific prohibition of an establishment of religion and introducing language that permitted religious taxation would be totally unacceptable to the Anifederalists. A conference committee was appointed – Madison, Sherman, and Vining represented the House – and on September 21 the Senate "receded" from its version of the Third Amendment and accepted the familiar language that was sent to the states on September 28, 1789, as Article III of the Bill of Rights: "Congress shall make no law respecting an establishment of religion, or prohibiting the free exercise thereof." The New England members of the House voted to accept this language, which can only mean that they were satisfied that the term "establishment of religion" permitted their states to lay and collect religious taxes without the threat of interference by agents of the national government. Whether the Antifederalists, who loathed religious taxes laid by any level of government, were aware that the phrase "establishment of religion" could be understood in this restricted sense is unclear. Senator Richard Henry Lee of Virginia complained to Patrick Henry in September that the Senate's objective in offering its amendments was to "produce ambiguity." The best guess – and it is only a guess – is that the establishment clause, as it related to religious taxation, may have been intended to be deliberately ambiguous, permitting the members to interpret it as it best suited their personal and regional interests.

Discerning the meaning of the religious language of the Third Amendment, which became the First Amendment after the states rejected the first two original amendments submitted to them, has become a cottage industry in the nation's law schools and history and political science departments as a result of decisions of the United States Supreme Court after World War II. The amendment was intended by Madison and his fellow drafters to make explicit the small *f* federalism on which the Constitution was grounded. The states had granted Congress no power over religion. The First Amendment was intended to declare this to be so. Clear language, affirming Congress's lack of power, was suggested by Samuel Livermore of New Hampshire during the August 15 debates: "congress shall make no law touching religion." Madison knew, however, that the Antifederalists, would not be satisfied with short, general statements. They wanted specifics, and specifics he gave them in introducing his religion amendments on June 8. His specifics survived the drafting process and emerged, in altered form, in the First Amendment, as the terms "establishment of religion" and "free exercises" of religion.

The debates in the First Congress on the religion clause of the Third, later First, Amendment are meager. There is no indication that any attempt was made to define an "establishment of religion," which, as stated earlier, may have been left deliberately ambiguous. In 1789 the most expansive American definition of the term would have included state regulation of its citizens' faith and practice and state imposition of taxes to pay ministers and build churches. Beyond these limits, most Americans would have granted the state considerable latitude in supporting religion. But this possibility was evidently not discussed in the First Congress. Members, for example, appear not to have tried to obtain clarification about whether the new national government could grant "friendly aids" to religious groups with the same generous hand that all agreed, during the debates on general assessment, the states could provide for churches within their boundaries. As incompetent as the shorthand reporters were, they surely would have produced some account, garbled or otherwise, of discussions of these and similar questions had they been raised during the First Congress. All indications are that in debating the religion clause of what became the First Amendment, Congress only considered the issue of federalism as it related to the propriety of religious taxes levied by the New England state governments. Congressmen, who did not think amendments necessary in the first place and who were impatient with the whole amending process, were unwilling to invest time in defining terms whose meaning is passionately contested by their posterity.

A debate in Congress on September 25, occurring, as it did, the day after the House adopted the amendments to the Constitution, sheds light on how the members regarded the religious language of the Third, later First, Amendment. On September 25, the pious Elias Boudinot, president of Congress, 1782–3, announced to his colleagues that he could not "think of letting the session pass without offering an opportunity to all citizens of the United States of joining, with one voice, in returning to Almighty God their sincere thanks for the many blessings that He poured down upon them." Boudinot moved, therefore, that the House and Senate request the president "to recommend to the people of the United States a day of public thanksgiving and prayer, to be observed by acknowledging, with grateful hearts, the many signal favors of Almighty God."

Thanksgiving and fast day proclamations soon became controversial, as John Adams discovered in 1798, because they were viewed by the emerging Jeffersonian Republican Party as instruments of partisan politics. In 1789, however, proclamations were considered to be as beneficial and unobjectionable as they had been for the past two centuries, even though they were acknowledged to be religious actions initiated by the executive branch of government. Because of the unimpeachable precedents for issuing proclamations, Boudinot may have been surprised, when two of his colleagues objected to his motion on the grounds that it violated the principle of federalism. Issuing a thanksgiving proclamation, Thomas Tucker of South Carolina complained, "is a business with which Congress have nothing to do; it is a religious matter, and, as such, is proscribed to us. If a day of thanksgiving must take place, let it be done by the authority of the several states."

Roger Sherman answered Tucker by observing that the "practice of thanksgiving [was] warranted by a number of precedents in the Holy Writ," which he commended as being "worthy of Christian imitation on the present occasion." Boudinot cited "further precedents from the practice of the late Congress" which, of course, had approved the wholesale issuance of thanksgiving and fast day proclamations. Boudinot's purpose in referring to practices in the Continental and Confederation Congresses was to make the point that under the Constitution, as well as under the Articles of Confederation, the national government could assume, without objection, that it possessed undelegated, inherent powers to conduct religious activities, which trumped the principle of federalism as well as the language of the just minted Third Amendment, prohibiting an establishment of religion. These powers included, at the very least, issuing religious proclamations and appointing military and civilian chaplains. They expanded during the Jefferson administration to the staging of religious services on public property. During the first years of the government under the Constitution, no attempt was made to define the limitations on these "friendly aids" to religion.

Boudinot's motion for a presidential proclamation passed both houses of Congress with only two recorded objections. On October 3, 1789, George Washington issued a proclamation recommending that the American people, on November 26, 1789, hold thanksgiving services to express their gratitude to God for his "signal and manifold mercies, and the favorable interpositions of his providence" as well as to beseech Him "to pardon our national and other transgressions."

The language concerning religion in the First Amendment to the Constitution (ratified with the other nine amendments on December 15, 1791) had almost no immediate impact on relations between government and religion at either the national or state level. Speaker of the House Frederick Muhlenberg of Pennsylvania wrote Benjamin Rush on August 18, 1789, of his hopes that the proposed amendments to the federal constitution might "perhaps be the Means of producing the much wished for Alterations & Amendments in our State Constitution." The Pennsylvania constitution of 1790 eliminated the test oath, imposed by the 1776 constitution, that compelled public officer holders to be Christians, although it required them to acknowledge the "being of a God and a future state of rewards and punishments." If this clause was inspired by action at the federal level, the model was Article VI of the federal constitution, not the First Amendment. Commenting on the South Carolina constitution of 1790, a scholar has asserted, without producing any evidence, that "the pressure on the convention to do away with all religious distinctions came from the favorable adoption of the First Amendment to the U.S. Constitution." Few other scholars have been bold enough to attribute any immediate influence to the First Amendment. The historian Michael Kammen has, in fact, argued that the Bill of Rights had no impact in the United States until 1939–41, the first years of the Second World War, when it was at last "discovered" by the American public.

In the early years of the nineteenth century a disengagement of government from religion occurred in the New England states, but this divorce owed nothing to the First Amendment; it was the result of the democratization of American society and of the dynamics of American religion, specifically, of the evangelical tsunami, the Second Great Awakening, which began during the presidency of John Adams. The Awakening started with revivals at the eastern and western extremities of the United States, which soon passed each other, heading in opposite directions. Evangelical energy began coursing through Connecticut in 1797, quickly spread through New England, and reached northeast Ohio by 1802. The western revival began at Gaspar River, Kentucky, in the summer of 1800 and moved east to North Carolina by 1801; by 1803 it had swept through the entire southern seaboard.

Although the Second Great Awakening in New England was led by disciples and descendants of Jonathan Edwards and occurred in the same area as the First Great Awakening, the ferment in distant Kentucky was closer in spirit to the earlier revival in the passions of its preachers, the unrestrained emotional responses of its audiences and the controversies it generated. The sober and decorous New England revivals were universally approved and continued in some locations for decades. Connecticut became so saintly that foreign visitors were happy to hurry through the "dullest, most disagreeable state in the union."

To critics, Kentucky seemed to be in a state of nonstop bedlam. The crowds in Kentucky, though they seemed prodigious to participants, were no bigger than some that George Whitefield had drawn sixty years earlier. But they looked different. First Great Awakening audiences usually came from towns and cities and convened on short notice. In Kentucky and in other frontier areas, the audiences came from great distances by wagon, packed with provisions to sustain families for several days. When assembled, usually in clearings in the wilderness, these conventions of frontier farmers became camp meetings – a unique American contribution to religious history.

The largest and most famous Kentucky camp meeting took place at Cane Ridge in Bourbon County in August 1801. As many as twenty-five thousand people (twelve times the population of Kentucky's largest city) may have met for marathon day–night services, conducted by more than a score of Presbyterian, Baptist, and Methodist ministers, using stumps and fallen logs for pulpits. "The noise," recalled a participant, "was like the roar of Niagara. The vast sea of human beings seemed to be agitated, as if by a storm." "At night," wrote another eye witness:

> the whole scene was awfully sublime. The ranges of tents, the fires, reflecting light amidst the branches of towering trees; the candles and lamps illuminating the encampment; hundreds moving to and fro, with lights and torches, like Gideon's army; the preaching, praying, singing and shouting, all heard at once, rushing from different parts of the ground, like the sound of many waters, was enough to swallow all powers of contemplation. Sinners falling, and shrieks and cries for mercy awakening in the mind a lively apprehension of the scene, when the awful sound will be heard, 'arise ye dead and come to judgment.'

Traditionalists charged that camp meetings had all the excesses of a 1960s rock concert, including sexual license. At the meetings, it was said, "more soul were begat than saved." Presbyterians and

Baptists renounced them. Embraced by the Methodists, they quickly became the ecclesiastical signature of that denomination. By 1805 Methodists had brought the camp meeting across the Alleghenies to Virginia. Three years latter, they conducted a "remarkable" revival in New York City, followed in the next decade by major revivals in Philadelphia, Baltimore, and Providence. Scholars credit the Methodists with bringing the "lusty breath of the western revival into the east," but they were assisted by preachers like the Presbyterian, Charles Grandison Finney, who used their "new measures" to conduct a major evangelical campaign in the big cities along the Atlantic Coast in the 1830s.

Finney's first successes occurred in that region of western New York known as the Burned Over District, because of the frequency with which it had been seared by the fires of revivalism. Between 1800 and 1830, the nation itself can be thought of as a giant burned over district, for during this period no region was too remote to have been at least singed by evangelical religion. Evangelicalism's hegemony in 1830 can be read in the membership roles of the nation's denominations. Those churches that embraced and sponsored revivalism dwarfed those that spurned it. The Baptists and Methodists were in a virtual dead heat in 1830 as the nation's largest denominations. Their growth rate was remarkable. The Methodists, for example, starting with fewer than 10,000 members in 1780, numbered 250,000 in 1820, doubled to 500,000 by 1830, and doubled again during the next decade to become, by 1844, the nation's largest denomination with 1,068,525 members.

The Second Great Awakening produced, as had the First, schisms among the major churches, which notably increased the pluralism of American religion. In addition, new religious groups like the Mormons appeared, whose origins were tangentially related to the

Awakening. American religion, according to one observer, now "had as many shades of difference as the leaves of autumn." Scholars have written that among the factors contributing to the multiplication of religious groups and opinions was the egalitarianism and jealousy fostered by revolutionary ideals which convinced the average citizen that his opinion on religious matters was as valid as those of the "experts." It was reported of one evangelical leader that "wherever he went, he industriously awakened the jealousy of the humble and ignorant against all men of superior reputation as haughty, insolent and oppressive."

By producing legions of Baptists and Methodist who were opposed in principle to tax support of religion and who, in addition, were generally "common men," suspicious of religious elites, the Second Great Awakening put the remnant of religious establishment in New England – the support of ministers and churches by taxation – on the path to extinction. Between 1816 and 1819 New Hampshire and Connecticut abolished religious taxation. Massachusetts resisted the tide until 1833, when it too abolished religious taxes. The last relic in America of the ancient, coercive Hildebrandine system had disappeared

But the abolition of religious taxes in favor of the reliance throughout the United States on voluntary, freewill financial support of churches did not mean that the states or the national government renounced other forms of government patronage of religion. It is true that the nursing fathers metaphor, with its talk of kings and queens, fell out of favor in the militantly republican atmosphere of early nineteenth-century America (it continued, nevertheless, to be used into the 1840s). The scriptural precept that the metaphor embodied, that the civil authorities should help their churches, continued to be honored, however, well beyond the Age of Jackson.

Professor John Witte has compiled a list of the "friendly aids" that the national and state governments offered to religion in the first half of the nineteenth century, which, although omitting incorporation and church services on public property, gives a good idea of the wide scope of this activity:

> Government officials . . . regularly acknowledged and endorsed religious beliefs and practices. "In God We Trust" and similar confessions appeared on currency and stamps. Various homages to God and religion appeared on state seals and state documents. The Ten Commandments and favorite Bible verses were inscribed on the walls of court houses, schools, and other public buildings. Crucifixes and other Christian symbols were erected in state parks and on state house grounds. Flags flew at half mast on Good Friday and other high holy days. Christmas, Easter, and other holy days were official holidays. Sundays remained official days of rest. Government-sponsored chaplains were appointed to Congress, the military, and various government asylums, prisons, and hospitals. Prayers were offered at the commencement of each session of Congress and of many state legislatures. Thanksgiving Day prayers were offered by presidents, governors, and other state officials. States underwrote the costs of Bibles and liturgical books for rural churches and occasionally donated land and services to them. Federal and state subsidies were given to Christian missionaries who proselytized among the native American Indians. Property grants and tax subsidies were furnished to Christian schools and charities. Special criminal laws protected the property and clergy of churches. Tax exemptions were accorded to the real and personal properties of many churches, clerics, and charities.

Witte and other scholars have asserted that this wide array of state support for religion (shorn of coercive laws assaulting the convictions and pocketbooks of individual citizens) amounted to a "de facto Christian establishment," an "informal Protestant establishment."

A major reason for public approval of multifaceted government support of religion was a broadly based concurrence in the ancient conviction that religion served the public good. By the third decade of the nineteenth century, more Americans than ever were prepared to acknowledge openly that this was so. Evangelicals had traditionally been reluctant to tout the public utility of religion for fear that their endorsement would recoil upon them. During the debates on general assessment in Massachusetts in the 1780s, Isaac Backus had more than once declared that "piety, religion, and morality are essentially necessary to the good order of civil society." He was challenged by opponents, who claimed that by acknowledging the public utility of religion, he was conceding the rationale for laying taxes to support it. William Gordon wrote in a Boston newspaper in May 1780 that, by endorsing public utility, Backus "gave up the whole cause for which he was Agent. Having allowed the premises, he could not appear with any consistency in opposition to the conclusions naturally and necessarily flowing from it." As the clock began to tick, ever louder, at the beginning of the nineteenth century, against religious taxation in its last New England citadels, this type of argument no longer had the power to intimidate evangelicals, and they began exuberantly asserting the public utility of religion, joining their voices to their former opponents to form a powerful national consensus on this point.

Nineteenth-century evangelical literature abounds with statements that could have been inspired by the religion section of Washington's Farewell Address or copied from the Massachusetts Constitution of 1780: "the religion of the Gospel is the rock on which civil liberty rests"; "civil liberty has ever been in proportion to the prevalence of pure Christianity"; "genuine religion with all its moral influences, and all its awful sanctions, is the chief, if not the only security we can have, for the preservation of free institutions"; "the doctrines of Protestant Christianity are the sure, nay, the only bulwark of civil freedom"; "Christianity is the only conservator of all that is dear in civil liberty and human happiness."

Evangelical petitions to Congress stressed these themes. One from a Vermont group in 1830 asserted, in the language of 1776, that "No Republican form of Government . . . can long exist in its original purity, without virtue & intelligence in the body politic . . . the principles and practice of the Christian Religion, unshackled by government, are the most effectual means of promoting & preserving that virtue and intelligence." To clinch their case, the pious petitioners added a paraphrase of Washington's Farewell Address.

For the evangelical community, the way to put these convictions into action, the means of becoming "doers of the word," was, of course, the promotion of revivals. "The preservation of our invaluable liberties and free institutions and all the happy prospects of our most favored country," wrote an evangelical spokesman in 1833, "depend greatly, under God, upon these pure and frequent and spreading revivals of religion, for which all American Christians of whatever names should pray."

Revivals proved their mettle in reforming social behavior throughout the country. A teacher traveling to Kentucky in 1802, at the peak of the revivals, was amazed at the transformation in what had been a brutal, lawless society: "I found Kentucky the most moral place I had ever been in," wrote the teacher, "a religious awe seemed to pervade the country." In South Carolina the same result was observed: "Drunkards have become sober and orderly – bruisers, bullies and blackguards meek, inoffensive and peaceable." Revivalists transformed the wayward into virtuous, law-abiding citizens by preaching the doctrine of a future state of rewards and punishments, a tactic considered for ages to be a foolproof method of creating good social behavior.

Fear of punishment, said one evangelical spokesman, must subdue the roughnecks populating the new republic and "no fear was strong enough but the fear of literal and everlasting burnings." James McGready, a leading western Presbyterian evangelist was admired for his ability "so to array hell before the wicked that they tremble and quake, imagining a lake of fire and brimstone yawning to overwhelm them and the hand of the Almighty thrusting them down the horrible abyss." More obscure exhorters used the same technique. Benjamin Henry Latrobe described a Methodist camp meeting outside Washington, D.C., in 1809, at which "Bunn the blacksmith" preached: "that's the pitch," bellowed Bunn, "the judgment to come, when the burning billows of hell wash up against the Soul" of the sinner; he has no power to "allay the fiery torment, the thirst that burns him, the parching that sears his lips . . . this is the judgement to come, when hell gapes, and the fire roars, Oh poor sinful damned souls, poor sinful souls all of ye, will ye be damned, will ye, will ye, will ye be damned!"

The evangelical community believed that the challenge to revivalism became more formidable with the acquisition of Louisiana in 1803 and with the rapid growth of urban America. Haunted for decades by the supposedly corrosive spiritual effects of western expansion, American religious leaders after 1803 saw beyond the Alleghenies an endless breeding ground for "violent and barbaric passions." Two missionaries who traveled to the farthest reaches of the Louisiana Territory in 1812 described their trip as an excursion into a moral "Valley of the Shadow of Death." The nation's growing cities were another source of anxiety, for they appeared to be filling up with a coarse rabble that might be indigestible by the nation's institutions. Evangelical religion alone seemed to be capable of implanting into these potentially dangerous populations that portion of virtue and morality needed to sustain a republican society and government.

To accomplish this goal, many of the nation's denominations surmounted the tensions within the evangelical camp, pooled their resources, and created institutions new to the country – the benevolent societies that, during the second decade of nineteenth century, began to blanket the land. These societies, which one scholar has called an "evangelical united front," were inspired by British examples and were the direct result of the extraordinary energies generated by the evangelical movement, specifically, by the "activism" resulting from conversion. "The evidence of God's grace," an evangelical spokesman insisted, "was a person's benevolence toward others."

Grounded in the churches, the benevolent societies usually operated as independent, ecumenical entities. The six largest societies in 1826–7 (based on their operating budgets) were all directly focused on conversion of souls: the American Education Society, the American Board of Foreign Missions, the American Bible Society, the American Sunday School Union, the American Tract Society, and the American Home Missionary Society. Three of these groups subsidized evangelical ministers, one specialized in evangelical education, and two supplied the literature that the other four used. The activity of these societies was feverish: During its first decade, the American Tract Society published and distributed thirty-five million pamphlets and books; in 1836 alone, the American Sunday School Union distributed seventy-three million pages of literature;

by 1826 the American Bible Society was publishing three hundred thousand bibles per year; and by 1831 the American Home Missionary Society had 463 missionaries in the field. So great was this pulsing energy that it extorted from a hostile observer, the Scottish freethinker, Fanny Wright, a backhand compliment on the success of the societies in clothing and feeding traveling preachers, "who fill your streets and highways with trembling fanatics, and your very forests with frantic men and hysterical women."

The benevolent societies and their supporting denominations were proud that, by converting their fellow countrymen, they made them good citizens; many, in fact, were boastful about what they considered the patriotic dimension of their work, using the term "patriotism" in its literal meaning of preserving the nation and its institutions. Consider the promotional literature distributed in 1826 by the American Home Missionary Society, whose records contain countless descriptions of the revivals conducted by its agents in the west and elsewhere. In 1826 the Society described how "feelings of Christian patriotism [were] excited and rendered ardent by the spiritual desolations which are seen to pervade many portions of our land." "More, much more," it asserted, "must be done by the sons of the Pilgrims and the servants of God, in the work of patriotism and Mercy." Make no mistake, the Society assured its readers, "we are doing the work of patriotism no less than Christianity and the friends of civil liberty may unite with all Christians and with the angels for the Agency of the Society. It has sought and, to no inconsiderable extent, it has already promoted, that intelligence and virtue without which civil liberty can not be maintained."

A few years later a convocation of the Episcopal Church received a similar message from one of its spokesmen: "we owe it to patriotism as well as to piety to keep the [missionary] system . . . should it cease . . . corruption and disorder will run riot over our country to the destruction of our civil and religious liberties . . . we must go forward for our country's sake as well as that of the church." Scripture was marshaled to support the synthesis of piety and patriotism; the apostle Paul, claimed a minister, was "one of the sublimest examples of patriotism ever exhibited to the world." But he was, another preacher pointed out, merely following the example of his Master, for "Jesus Christ was a patriot."

Missionary revivalism could support patriotism in other ways, its advocates contended. One was knitting together a society that showed signs of fragmenting, a task that many feared was beyond the capacity of the weak states-rights-oriented federal government of the early nineteenth-century republic. To Lyman Beecher, who recommended that "every man must be a revival man,"

> the prevalence of pious, intelligent, enterprising ministers throughout the nation, at the rate of one for a thousand, would establish . . . habits and institutions of homogeneous influence. These would produce a sameness of views, and feelings, and interests which would lay the foundation of our empire upon a rock. Religion is the central attraction which must supply the deficiency of political efficiency and interest.

Religion, in short, could be the "cement of civil society," a metaphor at least as old as the nursing fathers language.

In the first decades of the nineteenth century, evangelical America regarded itself (and was accepted by the nation's politicians) as a voluntary partner of a weak national government, operating in an area that was constitutionally off-limits – the formation of a national character sufficiently virtuous to sustain republican government – and in an area where the federal government was politically hamstrung – the creation of national unity. Saving souls, it was thought, would save the republic. This conviction commanded a consensus that extended from the floors of Congress to the nation's cities and farms to the humble colporteur tracking through the western wilderness with a saddlebag full of Bibles: all agreed that there must, as an 1826 sermon proposed, be an "association between Religion and Patriotism."

In the mid-1830s two observers, Charles Coffin and Alexis de Tocqueville, commented on the role of religion in the United States. Reverend Coffin, a New England-bred minister who followed a call to preach the gospel in Tennessee, is as obscure as Tocqueville is famous, but he was a thoughtful man who knew his country's history well. In 1833 he explained why the United States had been so hospitable to evangelicalism in general and revivalism in particular:

> never was there any other country settled, since Canaan itself, so much for the sacred purposes of religion, as our own. Never did any ancestry, since the days of inspiration, send up so many prayers and lay such ample foundations for the religious prosperity of their descendants, as did our godly forefathers. It is a fact, therefore, in perfect analogy with the course of Providence, that there never has been any other country so distinguished for religious revivals as our own.

At the same time that Coffin made these observations, Tocqueville was writing an account of his recent travels in the land of revivals that, when published in 1835 under the title of *Democracy in America*, became an instant classic. Everywhere he went in America, Tocqueville encountered the conviction, fostered by the evangelical juggernaut, that religion was essential to the political prosperity and durability of the republic and that there must, accordingly, be an "association" between it and government. Tocqueville, who rarely missed a trick, perceived the importance of this view, although he did not mention that it was an offspring of the revolutionary era conviction of the "public utility" of religion. Tocqueville recorded the public's opinion with his customary clarity:

> I do not know whether all Americans have a sincere faith in their religion; for who can search the human heart? But I am certain that they hold it indispensable to the maintenance of republican institutions. This opinion is not peculiar to a class of citizens or to a party, but it belongs to the whole nation, and to every rank of society.

The Tocqueville quotation is just the kind of penetrating statement that authors use to end their books. And it would have ended this book had Thomas Jefferson not written a letter some thirty years earlier that contained a controversial metaphor about the relationship between government and religion in the early republic that became a household expression in late twentieth-century America and that, as interpreted in various quarters, clashes with the conclusions reached in this book.

Inaugurated as the third president of the United States on March 4, 1801, Jefferson was immediately besieged with addresses of congratulations from supporters in all parts of the country. The nation's Baptists were overjoyed with the election of a man whom they had long regarded as a friend and ally. On October 7, 1801, members of the Danbury, Connecticut, Baptist Association sent Jefferson a letter congratulating him on his election, affirming their devotion to religious liberty and assailing the reactionary religious laws still on the books in Connecticut. The Baptists acknowledged that the federal nature of the American government prevented any direct presidential action to improve their local situation – they were "sensible," they said, "that the national government cannot destroy the Laws of each State" – but they hoped, nevertheless, that Jefferson's sentiments, "like the radiant beams of the Sun, will shine & prevail through all these States . . . till Hierarchy and tyranny be destroyed from the Earth."

Jefferson responded to the Danbury Baptists on January 1, 1802. In the course of his letter, he asserted that the religion section of the First Amendment – "Congress shall make no law respecting an establishment of religion, or prohibiting the free exercise thereof" – was intended to build a "wall of separation between Church & State." So slight was the impression made by the Danbury letter in 1802 and in the years immediately following that it was omitted from the first edition of Jefferson's collected works. The letter achieved publicity in legal circles in 1879, when it was quoted by Chief Justice Morrison Waite in his opinion in *Reynolds v. United States*, a case in which the Supreme Court decided that polygamy as practiced by the Mormons in Utah, in response to what they believed to be a divine revelation, was not protected as "free exercise" of religion under the First Amendment. Justice Waite quoted the wall of separation section of the Danbury Baptist letter, which was not, in fact, germane to his decision, based, as it was, on the distinction Jefferson made in the letter between religious opinions and actions stemming from them. The Danbury letter, opined Justice Waite, "may be accepted almost as an authoritative declaration of the scope and effect of the [first] amendment."

Despite Waite's salute to the Danbury letter, it retreated into the constitutional shadows until it was "rediscovered" by the Supreme Court in 1947, which turned the spotlight on the letter in *Everson v. Board of Education*, a case involving the constitutionality of public reimbursement of bus fares of students attending Catholic schools.

Speaking for a majority, which, it is often forgotten, approved the reimbursement, Justice Hugo Black wrote: "in the words of Jefferson, the clause [in the First Amendment] against the establishment of religion by law was intended to erect 'a wall of separation between church and state.'" "That wall" Black continued, "must be high and impregnable. We could not approve the slightest breach." The next year in another case about religion and the public schools, *McCollum v. Board of Education*, the Court "constitutionalized" Jefferson's wall metaphor, by asserting that it was the correct interpretation of the First Amendment's establishment clause. In subsequent decades, it employed the wall metaphor to strike down a number of venerable and cherished practices, such as prayer and Bible reading in the public schools, and various customary religious activities in pub-lic spaces, which, alternatively, thrilled and enraged opponents and proponents of these measures and made the "wall of separation" a familiar phrase. The *Everson* decision, predictably, became sub-ject of vitriolic controversy among lawyers, academics and partisan interest groups.

For an historian the intriguing feature of the *Everson* decision is the method Justice Black and his colleagues used to affirm that Jefferson, in writing to the Danbury Baptists in 1802, had correctly discerned the meaning of the First Amendment, passed in Congress thirteen year earlier when he was in France, where he could not have known what its drafters intended. The Justices used history to establish the meaning of the First Amendment and to confirm Jefferson's correct understanding of it. They wrote of finding the "meaning and scope of the First Amendment . . . in the light of its history." Justice Rutledge claimed that "no provision of the Con-stitution is more closely tied to or given content by its generating history than the religion clause of the First Amendment. It is at

once the refined product and terse summation of that history." Here
the Justices were following the strategy of Chief Justice Waite who
declared in *Reynolds* that, since the First Amendment was not self-
defining, "we must go, elsewhere, therefore, to ascertain its meaning,
and nowhere more appropriately, we think, than to the history of the
times in the midst of which the provision was adopted."

Justice Waite proceeded to provide a sketch of the history of
the government–religion question in the United States after 1776,
observing that the "controversy upon this general subject was ani-
mated, but seemed at last to culminate in Virginia," which led him to
focus on Madison's and Jefferson's roles in the conflict. In writing the
Everson opinion, Justice Black expanded on Waite's capsule history,
carrying the story back to the settlement of the American colonies
in the seventeenth century. Colonial Americans, Black wrote, experienced a "repetition of many of the old-world practices and persecutions," practices that became "so commonplace as to shock
the freedom loving colonists into a feeling of abhorrence." Assistance to religion proffered by their own governments aroused their
"indignation." "It was these feelings which found expression in the
First Amendment. No one locality and no one group throughout the
Colonies can rightly be given the credit for having aroused the sentiment that culminated in the adoption of the Bill of Rights provisions
embracing religious liberty." Black agreed with Justice Waite that
the movement for religious liberty reached its culmination in Virginia. "The people there, as elsewhere, reached the conviction that
individual religious liberty could be achieved best under a government which was stripped of all power to tax, support, or otherwise to
assist any or all religions." Virginia was represented as an uncom-
promising monolith in support of separation of church and state,
despite the fact that, had Patrick Henry not become governor in

1784, the state's assembly would have passed a bill, supported by John Marshall and George Washington, taxing its citizens to pay its preachers.

Black and his colleagues applauded the efforts of Jefferson and Madison to realize what they took to be the people's aspirations. Jefferson's Bill for Establishing Religious Freedom was quoted at length in the *Everson* decision; Madison's Declaration and Remonstrance of 1785 was reprinted in its entirety. These documents were considered as vehicles for the articulation of the popular demand for separation of church and state. Madison was considered to have incorporated the popular sentiments into the First Amendment in 1789. Since Jefferson's views, identical to Madison's, could also be considered to have been embedded in the First Amendment, he naturally knew its separationist purpose, which he conveyed to the Danbury Baptists in 1802. By deriving the meaning of the religion section of the First Amendment from the alleged strict separationist intentions of the American population, the Supreme Court in the *Everson* case, which was accused in this instance and in many others of an egregious abuse of its powers, ironically indulged in what opponents of "judicial activism" in the 1980s applauded as the "jurisprudence of original intention."

If there was a widespread popular demand in the 1770s and 1780s for the strict separation of church and state, as the Justice Black and his colleagues believed, the account given in this volume of the relationship between government and religion during these years is wrong. I have not found a scintilla of evidence that in the period after independence there was a popular groundswell for the separation of church and state. The opponents of government assistance to religion limited their demands to disestablishment, by which they meant the prohibition of coerced consciences and taxation to pay ministers' salaries. Beyond that, even the most resolute of former dissenters believed that there were plenty of ways in which the state could fulfill its old role of being, as the Presbyterians said, the nursing father of the church, thereby establishing what the Baptists agreed should be the "sweet harmony" between government and religion.

In 2002 the legal historian Philip Hamburger published a magisterial history of the concept of the separation of church and state in the United States, appropriately called *Separation of Church and State*, in which he established that not until the year 1800 was the concept introduced into American public discourse and then in the political arena by Jefferson's supporters trying to "browbeat the Federalist clergy from preaching about politics." As Hamburger traced the concept from its emergence in 1800 to its controversial career in the late twentieth century, he offered an explanation of what might have induced Justice Black in 1947 to discover separationist sentiment in the American population in the 1770s and 1780s. Hamburger demonstrated that the concept of the separation of church and state, as enunciated in Jefferson's letter to the Danbury Baptists, was distasteful to its Baptists recipients and gained little traction in the United States until, roughly, the Van Buren administration (1837–41), when it began to be employed to combat the massive influx of Catholic immigrants who, it was feared, would erect a Roman Catholic spiritual tyranny on the ruins of Protestantism. The concept thus became a shibboleth of nativists and anti-Catholics and eventually became a dogma of the Ku Klux Klan, a haven for both groups. Justice Black had been a Klansman as a young man, although he is credited with renouncing, later, the racism but not the anti-Catholicism of the "Invisible Empire."

The *Everson* case raised the issue of public funding for the Catholic Church, which Black, in obedience to his long-settled convictions, believed must be separated from the state. In *Everson*, Black sought to give the principle of separation of church and state historical corroboration by indulging in a species of judicial pseudo-scholarship, known in the legal fraternity as "law office history," which usually results, as a recent Chief Justice observed, in "bad history."

Practitioners of law office history are not interested in the complexities of the period they examine. They scan the historical record and select only those bits of evidence that will bolster their preconceived conclusions. Black's strategy – and here he was following the path Waite had taken in the *Reynolds* decision – was to concentrate on the church–state controversy in Virginia, on the grounds that it and its protagonists, Jefferson and Madison, fairly represented the views of the country at large (academic and other writers following in Black's footsteps as defenders of the principle of the separation of church and state often take the same approach when delving into the history of 1770s and 1780s). Black and his admirers viewed the nation as Virginia writ large and Madison as a tribune of the whole American people.

This is a gross misreading of the history of the postindependence period. Virginia, as this book has pointed out, was a special case. The Old Dominon was, in fact, unique among her sister colonies and, after 1776, states. She was the only colony to have sustained well into the eighteenth century the ancient ideal of uniformity of religion. When the perpetuation of uniformity was challenged in the 1760s, she was the only colony that experienced – and in most places condoned – massive and violent repression of the dissenters. The animosity that these events generated persisted after 1776 to a degree unequaled in the other states. Madison's reaction to the repression of the 1760s and 1770s was the cultivation of a settled hostility to the organized religion that appears to have been unique in America. He was the only politician in the nation who denied that religion had any "public utility." He was the only politician who opposed the appointment of legislative and military chaplains. He was the only major politician who opposed laws incorporating religious denominations. These and similar positions have prompted recent historians to describe Madison's views on the relationship between church and state as anomalous, "eccentric, and "radical." To claim that Madison's opinions on this subject represented those of his fellow citizens across the new republic is as farfetched as to assert that Voltaire's views on religion represented those of the Catholic hierarchy in France. Idiosyncratic personalities and events in Virginia cannot, in a word, be considered as surrogates for the United States in the first decades of the new republic.

As for the Danbury Baptist letter itself, Justice Black and his admirers were not in possession of evidence that became available in 1998 that demonstrated that in writing the letter Jefferson was interested less in making a general pronouncement about the relationship of government and religion than he was in explaining his position on a far narrower issue: the behavior of a republican chief executive. Jefferson's purpose in responding to the Danbury Baptists, he informed his attorney general, Levi Lincoln, on January 1, 1802, was to explain "why I do not proclaim fastings & thanksgivings, as my predecessors did," a practice that had become politically contentious during the Adams administration. In the fall of 1801, the proclamation problem reared its head again, when Jefferson refused to issue a Thanksgiving proclamation, praising God for the Treaty of Amiens between Great Britain and France, which saved the United States from being sucked into a devastating European war. The Federalists charged that Jefferson's delinquency was another example of his atheism, the alleged existence of which was the basis of their scurrilous campaign against him in the election of 1800. One of Jefferson's purposes in writing to the Danbury Baptists was to mount a political counterattack against the Federalists. The letter was meant to turn the tables on them by showing that their support for executive religious proclamations was another example of their unpatriotic thirst for the trappings of British monarchy, of their "Anglomania," of their Toryism.

As deleted and blotted out sections of the Danbury letter (recovered by the FBI in 1998) show, Jefferson intended to make his indictment of the Federalists stick by explaining the contrasting religious roles of the British monarch and the American president. He proposed to do this by using the ancient distinction – attributed by scholars to the fifth-century pope, Gelasius I – between the spiritual and temporal aspects of authority, between *sacerdotium* and *regnum*. It was a well-established principle of English law, a commentator wrote in 1713 in the *Codex Juris Ecclesiastici Anglicani*, that "England is governed by two distinct Administrations; one Spiritual, for matters of a Spiritual nature; and the other Temporal, for matters of a temporal nature." The King of England combined these two authorities in his own person, for, as another commentator wrote in 1679, he was a "mixed person." "*Rex Angliae est persona mixta, cum sacerdote*, say our Lawyers. He is a Priest as well as a King." As a priest–king, the British monarch was head of the Church of England and fully competent to perform ecclesiastical duties. Jefferson explained the propriety of the King of England's sacerdotal role in the blotted out section of the Danbury letter: "performances of devotion [can be] practiced indeed legally by the Executive of another nation as the legal head of a national church." The chief executive of the American republic could not, however, imitate the King of

England because the religion clause of the First Amendment had, in Jefferson's view, built a wall of separation between what in monarchical Europe had always been considered the chief magistrate's dual ecclesiastical and civil functions. The Bill of Rights, Jefferson believed, had debarred the president of the American republic from officiating in spiritual matters; "the duties of my station," he wrote, making the ancient distinction, "are merely temporal."

There was a political problem with the Danbury Baptist letter, as drafted, which Attorney General Lincoln spotted when Jefferson asked him to review it. By stigmatizing presidential proclamations as a tainted, Tory custom, the president risked offending New Englanders, Republicans, and "honest" Federalists alike, who, Lincoln reminded Jefferson, had "always been in the habit of observing fasts and thanksgivings in pursuance of proclamations of their respective executives" and who considered the custom as "venerable being handed down from our ancestors." Accordingly, Jefferson deleted those sections of the letter that could be interpreted as an "implied Censure" of proclamations, noting in the margin of the letter that they "might give uneasiness to some of our republican friends in the eastern states." In the process the president deprived future generations of the means of understanding the limited purpose he meant to achieve in the Danbury letter – distinguishing a republican from a monarchical chief executive – by using the phrase, wall of separation, in conjunction with the religion clause of the first Amendment.

Jefferson's refusal to issue proclamations continued to be fodder for his critics throughout his eight years as president. In January 1808 he sent the Reverend Samuel Miller a lengthy defense of his policy in which he raised the issue of federalism, of which he was a passionate advocate. Jefferson told Miller that the state governments, having reserved to themselves powers not granted to the national government in religious and other matters, might assist the cause of religion in ways that the national government could not. Although the president, in his view, could not issue religious proclamations, state governors might do so (as, in fact, Jefferson, as governor of Virginia, had done in November 1779, proclaiming a "Day of Solemn Thanksgiving and Prayer"). Jefferson did not comment on the wisdom of such policies, just as Madison had refrained from denouncing religious taxation in New England, which he tried to protect on the principle of federalism during the drafting of the First Amendment, however repugnant he personally considered the policy.

The edited Danbury letter, as sent to the Connecticut Baptists on January 1, 1802, lacked the explanatory power to blunt the Federalist criticism of Jefferson's refusal to issue religious proclamations. How could he publicly exonerate himself from their accusations of atheism? An opportunity presented itself on January 3, 1802, when Jefferson's old friend, John Leland, the Baptist preacher famous for the fervor of his evangelical preaching and his opposition to state support of religion, accepted an invitation to preach in the House of Representatives. "Contrary to all former practice," wrote a startled Federalist congressman, Jefferson appeared at church services in the House to hear Leland preach; Jefferson, in other words, attended an evangelical religious service and sung hymns, accompanied by the Marine Band, on public property two days after writing that the First Amendment erected a wall of separation between church and state, proof that he used the wall metaphor in the restrictive sense just described.

Jefferson's presence at Leland's service in the House, which generated nationwide publicity, as he must have anticipated, was not a one-time, cameo appearance. According to Margaret Bayard Smith, an early Washington insider, "Jefferson during his whole administration was a most regular attendant" at House services. There is abundant documentary evidence to support Mrs. Smith's claim. During Jefferson's presidency, Episcopal, Presbyterian, Quaker, Methodist, Baptist, and Swedenborgian ministers preached to congregations in the House, using the speaker's podium as their pulpit. On January 12, 1806, a female evangelist, Dorothy Ripley, entreated Jefferson, Vice President Aaron Burr, and a "crowded" House audience to open themselves to the necessity of the new birth. Services in the House continued until after the Civil War.

Those Federalists, who asserted that Jefferson's worshipping in the House on January 3, 1802, was sudden and unexpected, were wrong. During the preceding Congress (which assembled for the first time in Washington in the fall of 1800), Thomas Claggett, the chaplain of the Senate, told a friend that Jefferson, then vice president, "very constantly attended prayers every morning and . . . a course of Sermons which I have delivered in the Capitol on the truth of the Divine System." Afer he left public office and retired to Virginia, Jefferson constantly attended "union services," leadership of which rotated weekly between Presbyterians, Episcopalians, Baptists, and Methodists, at the Albemarle County Court House, arriving from Monticello with a "portable chair" and a prayer book.

Jefferson did more than passively attend religious services on public property. He permitted executive branch buildings, the War Office and the Treasury, to be used for services by local and visiting preachers, requiring, of course, that the structures be made available on an equal, nondiscriminatory basis. The first services at these sites, beginning in May 1801, were conducted by Baptists and Episcopalians. A Presbyterian clergyman, the Reverend James

Laurie, frequently preached at the Treasury. Laurie was a favorite of New Englanders. One of them, Manasseh Cutler, described a "very solemn," four-hour communion service in the Treasury, at which Laurie officiated just before Christmas in 1804. In 1806 John Quincy Adams inscribed a diary entry about the same Laurie as he ministered to an overflow audience in the Supreme Court chambers, a popular preaching venue during the Jefferson and Madison administrations.

Jefferson's patronage of religion during his presidency, which also included authorization of government funding for the Catholic Church's missionary efforts among the western Indians, demonstrates that his views about the relationship between government and religion were not, after all, that different from those of the great majority of his fellow citizens, although the extent of the "friendly aids" that he was prepared to offer to the country's churches was certainly near the low end of the national scale. Still, there is no reason to doubt the accuracy of a Jeffersonian anecdote recorded by a nineteenth-century Washington pastor. Walking to church in the Capitol one Sunday morning "with his large red prayer book under his arm," Jefferson responded to an acquaintance, skeptical about his destination, in the following manner: "no nation has ever yet existed or been governed without religion. Nor can be. The Christian religion is the best religion that has been given to man and I as chief Magistrate of this nation am bound to give it the sanction of my example."

Here was an articulation of what Justice Joseph Story in 1833 called "the general, if not universal, sentiment in America . . . that Christianity ought to receive encouragement from the State" because it promoted the public welfare, specifically, the "political prosperity" that Washington mentioned in his Farewell Address. These two ideas, that religion served the "public utility" and that it ought, accordingly, to be supported by the state (to the extent that the political culture permitted) were ancient; the rulers of Babylon and the Pharaohs of Egypt knew them and practiced upon them.

The other two major ideas about the relationship of religion and government, to which Americans subscribed in the Age of Jackson, were merely old, ushered into the world by small groups of courageous men and women – principally Anabaptists – during the Protestant Reformation of the sixteenth century. These ideas were the liberty of conscience and voluntarism. Liberty of conscience (more narrowly defined, to be sure, than twenty-first-century libertarians would prefer) was achieved in all American colonies save Virginia before the independence was declared in 1776. The American Revolution expanded its definition and anchored it unshakeably everywhere in the new nation. Voluntarism, the principle that religion must receive its financial support from freewill offerings of individuals not through state coercion in the form of taxes, was the exception rather than the rule in colonial America. It was a bitterly contested issue in the years immediately following the Revolution and did not prevail throughout the union until 1833.

The principal ideas about the relationship between religion and government to which the American nation subscribed in the 1830s were, respectively, three thousand and three hundred years old. If the American Revolution introduced into American life new ways of thinking about things and new ways of doing them – which it indisputably did – its innovative impulse produced little novelty in the realm of religion and government. There, in the years after the Revolution, ancient ideas thrived, and old ones were brought to fruition.

Bibliography

Bonomi, Patricia. *Under the Cope of Heaven: Religion, Society, and Politics in Colonial America.* New York: Oxford University Press, 2003.

Bonomi, Patricia, and Peter Eisenstadt. "Church Adherence in the Eighteenth-Century British American Colonies." *William and Mary Quarterly* 39, no. 2 (April 1982): 245–86.

Brant, Irving. *James Madison,* 6 vols. Indianapolis: Bobbs-Merrill, 1941–61.

Breen, T. H. *The Character of a Good Ruler: A Study of Puritan Political Ideas in New England, 1630–1730.* New York: Norton, 1974.

Brinsfield, John Wesley. *Religion and Politics in Colonial South Carolina.* Easley, S.C.: Southern Historical Press, 1983.

Buckley, Thomas E., S. J. *Church and State in Revolutionary Virginia, 1776–1787.* Charlottesville: University Press of Virginia, 1977.

Butler, Jon. *Awash in a Sea of Faith: Christianizing the American People.* Cambridge, Mass.: Harvard University Press, 1990.

Butterfield, Herbert. *The Whig Interpretation of History.* New York: AMS Press, 1978.

Chadwick, Owen, and Nuttall, Geoffrey. *From Uniformity to Unity.* London: S.P.C.K., 1962.

Clark, J. C. D. *English Society, 1688–1832: Religion, Ideology, and Politics during the Ancien Regime.* New York: Cambridge University Press, 2000.

Curry, Thomas J. *The First Freedoms: Church and State in America to the Passage of the First Amendment*. New York: Oxford University Press, 1986.

Davies, Paul C. "The Debate on Eternal Punishment in Late Seventeenth and Eighteenth Century England." *Eighteenth Century Studies* 4, no. 3 (Spring 1971): 257–76.

Davis, Derek. *Religion and the Continental Congress, 1774–1789*. New York: Oxford University Press, 2000.

Dreisbach, Daniel L. *Religion and Politics in the Early Republic: Jasper Adams and the Church–State Debate*. Lexington: University Press of Kentucky, 1996.

Dunn, Mary M., and Richard S. Dunn, eds. *The Papers of William Penn*, 4 vols. Philadelphia: University of Pennsylvania Press, 1981–87.

Edwards, Morgan. *Materials towards a History of the Baptists*. Danielsville, Ga.: Heritage Press, 1984.

Gaustad, Edwin S. *Sworn on the Altar of God: A Religious Biography of Thomas Jefferson*. Grand Rapids, Mich.: W.D. Eerdmans, 1996.

Grell, Ole, et. al., eds. *From Persecution to Toleration: The Glorious Revolution and Religion in England*. New York: Oxford University Press, 1991.

Hamburger, Philip. *Separation of Church and State*. Cambridge, Mass.: Harvard University Press, 2002.

Holmes David. *The Religion of the Founding Fathers*. Charlottesville, Va.: Ash Lawn and the William L. Clements Library, 2003.

Hoppit, Julian. *A Land of Liberty? England, 1689–1727*. New York: Oxford University Press, 2000.

Hutson, James H. *Religion and the Founding of the American Republic*. Hanover, N.H.: University Press of New England, 2002.

   Forgotten Features of the Founding: The Recovery of Religious Themes in the Early American Republic. Lanham, Md.: Rowman & Littlefield, 2003.

   The Founders on Religion: A Book of Quotations. Princeton, N.J.: Princeton University Press, 2005.

Jordan, Wilbur K. *The Development of Religious Toleration in England from the Beginning of the English Reformation to the Death of Queen Elizabeth*. London: G. Allen & Unwin, 1932.

The Development of Religious Toleration in England from the Accession of James I to the Convention of the Long Parliament, 1603–1640. Cambridge, Mass.: Harvard University Press, 1936.

The Development of Religious Toleration in England from the Convention of the Long Parliament to the Restoration, 1640–1660. London: G. Allen & Unwin, 1938.

Ketcham, Ralph. *James Madison: A Biography*. New York: Macmillan, 1971.

Kramnick, Isaac, and Laurence R. Moore. *The Godless Constitution: The Case against Religious Correctness*. New York: W.W. Norton Publishers, 1996.

Lambert, Frank. *The Founding Fathers and the Place of Religion in America*. Princeton, N.J.: Princeton University Press, 2003.

Levy, Leonard. *Blasphemy: Verbal Offense against the Sacred, from Moses to Salman Rushdie*. New York: Knopf, 1993.

Establishment Clause: Religion and the First Amendment. Chapel Hill: University of North Carolina Press, 1994.

Little, Lewis Peyton. *Imprisoned Preachers and Religious Liberty in Virginia*. Lynchburg, Va.: J.P. Bell Co., 1938.

McLoughlin, William. *Isaac Backus on Church, State, and Calvinism*. Cambridge, Mass.: Harvard University Press, 1968.

New England Dissent, 1630–1833, 2 vols. Cambridge, Mass.: Harvard University Press, 1971.

Meacham, Jon. *American Gospel: God, the Founding Fathers, and the Making of a Nation*. New York: Random House, 2006.

Miller, Perry. *The New England Mind: The Seventeenth Century*. Cambridge, Mass.: Harvard University Press, 1954.

The New England Mind: From Colony to Province. Cambridge, Mass.: Harvard University Press, 1983.

Roger Williams: His Contribution to the American Tradition. Indianapolis: Bobbs-Merrill, 1954.

Morgan, Edmund S. *The Puritan Dilemma: The Story of John Winthrop.* Boston: Little, Brown, 1958.

    Roger Williams; The Church and State. New York: Harcourt, Brace, 1964.

    American Slavery, American Freedom: The Ordeal of Colonial Virginia. New York: Norton, 1975.

Nelson, John K. *A Blessed Company: Parishes, Parsons, and Parishioners in Anglican Virginia, 1690– 1776.* Chapel Hill: University of North Carolina Press, 2001.

Noonan, John T. *The Lustre of Our Country: The American Experience of Religious Freedom.* Berkeley: University of California Press, 1998.

Novak, Michael, and Jana Novak. *Washington's God: Religion, Liberty, and the Father of Our Country.* New York: Basic Books, 2006.

Penn, William. *The Select Works of William Penn*, 3 vols. New York: Kraus Reprint Company, 1971.

Pratt, John W. *Religion, Politics, and Diversity: The Church–State Theme in New York History.* Ithaca, N.Y.: Cornell University Press, 1967.

Reese, Thomas. *An Essay on the Influence of Religion in Civil Society.* Charleston, S.C.: Markland and McIver, 1788.

Sandoz, Elliot, ed. *Political Sermons of the American Founding Era 1730–1805.* Indianapolis: Liberty Press, 1991.

Stark, Rodney, and Roger Finke, "American Religion in 1776: A Statistical Portrait." *Sociological Analysis* 49, no. 1 (1988): 39–51.

Sykes, Norman. *Church and State in England in the 18th Century.* New York: Octagon Books, 1975.

Thornton, John W. *The Pulpit of the American Revolution.* New York: Burt Franklin, 1970.

Tully, James. "Governing Conduct." Pp. 289–348 in *Locke Volume II*, edited by John Dunn and Ian Harris. Cheltenham, U.K.: Edward Elgar Publishing Limited, 1997.

Veit, Helen, et. al., eds. *Creating the Bill of Rights.* Baltimore: Johns Hopkins University Press, 1991.

Viner, Jacob. *The Role of Providence in the Social Order*. Philadelphia: American Philosophical Society, 1972.

Walker, Daniel P. *The Decline of Hell: Seventeenth-Century Discussions of Eternal Torment*. Chicago: University of Chicago Press, 1964.

Watts, Michael R. *The Dissenters*. Oxford: Clarendon Press, 1978.

Williams, Roger. *The Complete Works of Roger Williams*, 7 vols. New York: Russell and Russell, 1963.

Zagorin, Perez. *How the Idea of Religious Toleration Came to the West*. Princeton, N.J.: Princeton University Press, 2003.

Index